More Memories of
of
Sunderland

The publishers would like to thank the following companies for their

support in the production of this book

Main Sponsor

Rolls-Royce Plc

George V Cummins Limited

H Jones & Sons Grocers Limited

Tenon Jennings Johnson

Fred Stoddart Limited

Port of Sunderland

University of Sunderland

First published in Great Britain by True North Books Limited
England HX5 9AE
01422 377977

ISBN 1 903204 48 8

Text, design and origination by True North Books Limited
Printed and bound by The Amadeus Press Limited

More Memories of Sunderland

Contents

Beamish Museum

Introduction

Once upon a time there was a land where Brownies wore berets instead of baseball caps, Victorian architecture was considered more attractive than steel and glass, a family ate its tea together at a table and shipbuilding provided employment for all. That land was called Britain and it is to a particular part of our noble isle that we are about to return in 'More Memories of Sunderland', a journey through the city that time has not forgotten, but there is a danger that modern society will. Within the pages of this book the reader will find a photographic and textual stimulus to the life and times of the last century that are the heritage of us all. We will have lived through parts of that era, but our parents and grandparents will have contributed personally to the earlier pictures that are painted by word or image. The book is not meant to be a definitive history, but a nostalgic looking back at buildings, events and places that are no longer with us or whose nature has changed as the years have rolled by. Everyone reading 'More Memories of Sunderland' will be able to associate with the scenes that unfold as each page is turned and reminisce about the good times that were had or that have been alluded to by our older relatives. Each lovely photograph inside is annotated with a caption that adds to the impact the image makes by highlighting certain elements or reminiscing about how life was when variety was king or long playing records were first placed on a turntable. Not everything in a nostalgic review is wonderful, for some of the old days were not as good as we might be led to think and this book does not duck the more painful issues. We return to the war years as well as the swinging 60s and revisit the decline of the shipyards whilst shopping again at H Binns, Son & Co Ltd.

Although within the reader will find the 20th century revisited, it is important to remember that Sunderland's heritage goes back much further than that captured on film. On 23 March 1992 it was elevated to city status, as befits a vibrant conurbation of nearly 300,000, when the Queen decided to commemorate 40 years on the throne, but it would once have been home to a handful of hunter gatherers until the Celts arrived.

Children and adults meeting the animals at Durham County Show

Beamish Museum

Evidence of their presence can be gained from the name of our river, for 'Wear' is a Celtic word that means 'water' or, possibly, 'river'. There is only minimal proof that the Romans had much contact with the immediate area and it is not until the arrival of Anglo Saxon tribes that the real history of the city begins. The first records credit Benedict Biscop, a Northumbrian nobleman, with establishing a monastery on the banks of the Wear in 674 AD. The famous historian, the Venerable Bede, studied there, but invading tribes had no sense of its importance and the ninth century Vikings and 11th century Scots both sacked the monastery. During medieval times two communities developed at the port of Wearmouth and Bishop-wearmouth and it was around this time that Sunderland's name was coined, meaning 'separate land' or 'sundered land' as it was across the river from Monkwearmouth. By the end of the 14th century coal was being shipped along the river and one of the country's first shipbuilding industries was established. In Jacobean times coal pits were sunk near the Wear and quays built to facilitate movement of coal and salt from the nearby pans. In the 1700s the harbour was greatly improved and the growth in trade associated with the ship and

boat yards encouraged industries such as rope and sailmaking to flourish. By the time Queen Victoria ascended the throne the volume of Sunderland's shipbuilding equalled the total output of the rest of the country, making it the world's largest such town. Railway links to the collieries, a burgeoning reputation for pottery and glass and the continued success of the shipyards helped its importance in the nation's economy to grow even further, so that by 1888 it had become a county borough. In 1801 Sunderland's population stood at just over 12,000, but it increased by more than tenfold during the 19th century, bringing changes which have a meaning for us today in understanding the layout of our city and dedication of some of its streets and place names. The Fawcett family estate was used to provide prestigious homes for the prosperous middle classes, with the main street bearing the family name and neighbouring ones being given other titles that could be linked to the Fawcetts, as in John Street, Frederick Street and Foyle Street. Gradually, in order to be closer to a valuable clientele, shops and offices began to creep ever further from around and along High Street to take up positions on Fawcett Street itself.

Holmeside pictured in the early 1950s.

The majestic Town Hall was built, further marking the importance of this part of Sunderland. At the same time, the working classes were accommodated in Sunderland cottages north of the river on streets named after politicians of the day, Selbourne, Bright, Hartington, Cardwell etc. Similar dwellings were erected south of the river in Millfield, providing the unfortunate potential for those properties to be condemned as slums in the 20th century. Further change to the fabric of society took place after the 1914-18 war when shipbuilding went into dramatic decline, taking with it other related industries that depended upon it for their very existence. In 1960 coal mining employed over 18,000 local workers, but that industry continued its slide into oblivion, culminating in the closure of Wearmouth Colliery in 1993. In the meantime, to redress the balance, the Nissan car plant had come to the area and business parks and enterprise centres established to meet the technological demands of the 21st century.

Having set the scene, it is now time to delve into a feast of memories and half forgotten experiences as you turn the first page that will unleash wave after wave of nostalgia for days that are only just around the corner, but were lived at a slower pace and in a different style. Go back in time to when metal tubes containing a shopper's money whizzed through the air on a journey to the cashier's booth and then back again with the change. Drive a Ford Prefect along John Street without being flattened in the bus lane or reach into your pocket for a half crown with which to buy a round of drinks at the Boilermakers' Arms on High Street West. Take a tram ride to Roker Pier and put a hankie on your head as you sit on a deck chair on the sands, baking in the sun, braces hanging freely. Ask yourself if Billy Fury ever got further than halfway to paradise or did the Andrews Sisters eventually see someone else under that apple tree. As you enter the world that 'More Memories of Sunderland' will bring why not suck on a Spangle or chew on a stick of licorice root? Put some coal on the fire and let the smoke billow forth from the chimney as you listen to Mrs Mop asking Tommy Handley, 'Can I do you now, sir?' on the wireless. Draw the blackout curtains and light up a fag from a packet of Player's Weights. You are about to be whisked off on a voyage to an era that will never return, but one that has touched us all.

Street scenes

Beamish Museum

The shiny black motor cars lined up outside Binns, Sunderland's premier department store, on Fawcett Street take us back to television and movie images of 'The Untouchables', the popular story of Eliot Ness and his police squad who fought the Chicago mobsters during the prohibition era in America. You can almost see men jumping onto running boards as cars roared down the street, machine guns blazing away. Although the date of this picture, c1930, is about right Sunderland never descended into the depths of mob rule that afflicted the States, even if it did have one or two less than salubrious areas in the town. That could not be said of Fawcett Street, for it had long had the reputation of being one of the finer districts of Sunderland. Named after the prosperous family on whose estate many handsome streets and good middle class housing were laid out, it developed further into being a major focus as a shopping centre. The number of cars indicates the prosperity of those who visited the district, because they were largely restricted to ownership by the well to do. Beyond Binns, on the left, the Town Hall, designed by Brightwen Binyon of Ipswich, stood as a significant landmark. It was opened on 6 November 1890, but was sacrificed to progress by the vandals who called themselves town planners in 1971, being demolished a year after the completion of the new Civic Centre opposite Mowbray Park.

Right: The couple on the left of this view of Burleigh Street in the 1930s was only a cobbled street's width from the residents on the right, but their dress suggests that they were worlds apart. He is nattily attired in his suit and raincoat and his companion is fashionably dressed in a smart topcoat and elegant shoes, whilst the women outside their front doors could almost be from another planet. The older ones are encased in shawls and black, serviceable clothing favoured by the elderly of the time, with the younger housewives dressed in frocks they made themselves from cheap material purchased with money scrimped and saved from the housekeeping money. There is almost an air of hostility that can be detected coming from the woman with her arms folded as she stares across at the couple on the corner. In the 1930s the class structure was still very much an integral part of society and dividing lines were clearly drawn. The have nots despised their social betters, whilst the latter looked down on the working classes. It took the war to begin the process of breaking down those barriers that had partitioned our society for too long, but it was a costly and painful way of achieving something that should have been done away with if only our forebears had been blessed with greater tolerance and less fear of relinquishing the power that came with wealth.

Below: It is not clear what the bowler hatted gentleman was doing on Burleigh Street as he chatted to the householders, ready in their pinnies to undertake another dose of the daily grind of washing, cleaning and cooking that seemed to fill their lives in those days. However, it is likely that his home was some distance from the east end of the town and that he had called on these women as part of his job or business. If he had called to collect the rent then he was in luck as the door had been answered to him. There were some houses that he visited where no response could be gained, mainly because the holder of the family purse was short that week and had taken refuge behind the kitchen door, away from prying eyes looking through the window or peering through the letter box. Sometimes a young child would appear in the doorway and tell him that mum had gone out, but then spoil the subterfuge by turning round and shouting 'Haven't you, mam?' Others knocking on the door included moneylenders who had helped tide a family over a particularly bad patch, but whose interest rates meant that the period of repayment stretched far into the distance. The lucky residents were those who had bought something from a salesman and were able to pay off their debt in reasonable weekly instalments whilst enjoying the benefits of what they had purchased.

It must have been a chilly day in 1938 to judge from the way shoppers were dressed as they stood outside Binns on Fawcett Street, as viewed from the traffic lights at the junction with Borough Road. Perhaps the January sales were on, attracting custom from both within and outside Sunderland in the chance of grabbing a bargain. The women were well wrapped up in long coats, some of them made of fur that would have the animal rights lobby in uproar today. How times change, for look at the male and female headwear on display and take a stroll along here today to see whether or not you can see anybody wearing a fashionable hat of any description. Modern fashion seems to have relegated fancy headgear to weddings and garden parties, but at one time it was in everyday use. Other styles have moved on as well and apparel such as the plus fours worn by the man crossing the road can only be seen today on the occasional hiker or Payne Stewart look alike golfer. Over to the right we can just make out a man wearing a sandwich board that would have been used for a variety of purposes. On one day it would have advertised the latest show at the Empire, on another a sale at a department store or even been used to warn that the end was nigh, so sinners had better repent.

Many of the streets on either side of Chester Road were laid out in straight lined grids in the 1880s and provided homes for skilled workers and the lower middle classes. Chester Road was also home to the workhouse that in Victorian times accommodated 500 people and had its own schools and farm. The General Hospital now stands on the same site. This scene from the 1940s offers a strange picture of police activity. Traffic was being carefully orchestrated by the bobby in the centre of the road as he ushered the woman across

Beamish Museum

whilst he kept the buses at bay. But, take a good look at his colleague, beside the roadworks. He appears to be engrossed in a book, but perhaps he could have convinced onlookers that he was merely swotting up on some point from his police manual. Whatever it is that has transfixed him goes to show that it is not only road repairers who can take it easy, as shown by the two on the left. One has a nonchalant hand in his pocket as his workmate leans on a shovel. This was not going to be a day when too many holes would be dug nor criminals caught if the activity on view was any measure.

Never were eyes in the back of his head more needed by anyone than in the case of the policeman on point duty on Holmeside, where it meets Crowtree Road and Park Lane, for he was in dire danger of being flattened by the oncoming tram approaching from Borough Road, to the east. Presumably, his ears alerted him in time because the clanking tram was not the quietest of vehicles on our roads in those days, though the rattle of Magog's removal van would have provided some cover if the tram driver had an evil streak to his nature! Today, to the left we can find Debenham's and an entrance to the Bridges Shopping Centre, whilst, on the right, there is Liberty's Bar in the building that became the ABC and the Cannon, but was known to older Sunderland cinemagoers as the Ritz. It opened on the site of a former cattle market on 1 March 1937, showing one of Fred Astaire and Ginger Rogers' musicals 'Swing Time'. It was not one of their best efforts, but it included 'The way you look tonight', a song that was to become a classic standard. The movie showing when this scene was captured, 'The Duke of West Point', was made in 1938, starring Louis Hayward and Joan Fontaine. It was a rather dated flagwaver about an extrovert army cadet who found the going tough.

Left: George Binns founded a modest drapery business on High Street in 1807, but it is the department store on Fawcett Street, established by his grandson JJ Binns that we all remember with great affection. By the early days of the 20th century its array of London and Paris fashions and elegant costumes had attracted such a reputation for excellence that the store became like Topsy as it just 'growed and growed'. Neighbouring premises were taken over until the floor space totalled some two acres patrolled by over 400 employees. It was the premier shopping experience in Sunderland and only the bombs dropped by enemy aircraft during World War II interrupted its business. The store was badly damaged, but from the ashes rose a new five storey building that opened for business on 2 March 1953, shortly before this photograph was taken from a vantage point on the museum roof. Binns became part of the House of Fraser empire and continued to expand, but as there was no room for further growth on this side of Fawcett Street, in 1958 it simply started building another branch on the opposite side of the road. Connected to the main building by a subway, the extension opened its doors to the public in 1962. Sunderland shopping without Binns just does not seem the same any more as the unimaginable took place when the tills stopped ringing and, first of all the newer section closed in April 1989, to be followed by the main store on Saturday 30 January 1993.

Above: To be a successful photographer you need to have a mental image of the shot you are trying to take and good quality equipment to ensure that the scene is faithfully captured. There is something else required, namely a head for heights, as no sufferer from vertigo would have enjoyed climbing onto the roof of Binns department store to commit this 1953 scene to film. Blandford Street runs away west towards Maritime Terrace and Crowtree Road, parallel to Brougham Street and Holmeside that flank it right and left. Traffic no longer runs along here for it is now part of the pedestrianised area that leads towards the Bridges Shopping Centre. As the photographer looked across Waterloo Place to take his photograph the very name of that street reminded him of the importance Victorians gave to military events and heroes of the 19th century. The Duke of Wellington has some connection with Sunderland because his brother Gerald served as the Rector of Bishopwearmouth for over 20 years from 1827. The Duke had several other titles, including the Marquis of Douro, and Douro Terrace, the short stretch of road running away beyond the Civic Centre from the south west corner of Mowbray Park, is a less known link with the soldier who had a brief and undistinguished spell as our prime minister.

The Wearmouth bridges have a history that dates back to the 18th century as the foundation stone for the first bridge at this spot was laid on 24 September 1793, though it was not until 9 August 1796 that the first carts drove across the 236 foot long brainchild of financier and part designer Rowland Burdon. With a width of 32 feet it was a marvel of modern engineering as the world's largest single arch cast iron bridge, though it required some strengthening in 1805. It had a clearance of 100 feet above the river, enabling easy movement beneath it as port traffic increased through the 19th century with paddle steamers a familiar sight. The complete rebuilding of the bridge was overseen by Robert Stephenson, the man responsible for the Britannia Bridge over the Menai Strait, shortly before his death in 1859. The railway bridge was added 20 years later, linking what had been two separate networks for North East Railways. Development along the Wear had been in an east to west movement, but the access across the river assisted in extending Sunderland's growth in a north to south pattern. This view was taken from the Lambton west coal staithes in 1968, by which time the view had changed again since the opening of the new road bridge in 1929.

Beamish Museum

Events & occasions

Beamish Museum

Southwick was an area where once you could find a variety of work in its lime kilns, quarries, potteries and shipyard. William Pickersgill built his yard here in 1836 and, even as late as 1943, the Shipbuilding Corporation opened a yard in response to wartime demands. However, it was to a different war that this photograph is dedicated, having been taken as a street party was about to be held to celebrate the armistice in 1918. Flags and decorations, locked away since the coronation of George V, flew across the street and from every window as people breathed a sigh of relief that four terrible years had come to an end. The government promised that there would be a land fit for heroes in the future and, rather naively, it was believed. Tragically, so many of those heroes would never see any sort of tomorrow as they lay in the poppy fields and trenches of Ypres, Passchendaele, Mons and Verdun. They had marched off in 1914 singing 'It's a long way to Tipperary' and expecting to be back home by Christmas. The horrors that they experienced left even the survivors so mentally scarred that many refused to speak of their time at the front, even to their nearest and dearest. It was the children who particularly enjoyed the street parties, but this photograph acts as a poignant reminder that the early 20th century was not a comfortable time for the less well off. Standards of health and living conditions were poor, leading to sickness and disease that might have contributed to the plight of the youngster in the centre of the scene.

Below: Life might have been tough in this part of town, but that never stopped eastenders enjoying themselves when the opportunity arose. A national celebration was meant for the poor as well as the rich and who is to say who had the greater satisfaction from the decorations on display and the parties that were held in honour of a royal event. People on Burleigh Street might have been poor, but they were proud of their country and its monarchy, even if they had only the vaguest notion of how it operated. Union flags fluttered from windows and lines of brightly coloured bunting, made from scraps of old material, were strung from house to house across opposite sides of the street. In the mid 1930s there were two occasions when the nation let its hair down and forgot about the economic problems at home and the diplomatic ones abroad. On 6 May 1935 the nation revelled in the silver jubilee celebrations for King George V and gave three cheers for the 25 years of glorious rule. Without the benefit of television the residents of Burleigh Street could only imagine the huge crowds and the merriment around Nelson's Column or the sight of an elegant Queen Mary, resplendent in her necklace of pearls and brilliant white toque. But that did not stop them raising a glass of good cheer, something that was repeated two years later as the flags and bunting were pressed into service once again when George VI was crowned in Westminster Abbey.

The Duke of York, the future King George VI, inspected the guard of honour that had formed to greet him as he prepared to perform the ceremonial opening of the new Wearmouth Bridge in 1929. The bunting and union flags flying above his head marked the significance of his royal visit, but he little realised that it would fly again in his honour seven years later when he became king. When the final ceremonial silver rivet was installed and he opened the bridge, designed by Mott, Hay and Anderson, his brother was expected to succeed George V eventually, but he only did so for less than a year before abdicating. If the shy Duke of York had known in 1929 that he would have to pick up the reins of monarchy he might have been tempted to drown his sorrows in Bridge End Vaults, at the top right of the photograph. The pub had undergone extensive renovations in 1890, made doubly so when the whole structure collapsed leaving a scene of devastation in its wake. Rebuilt, it provided sustenance for princes and paupers until October 1967 when landlady Ann Thompson pulled her last pint and knocked the final top off a bottle of Double Diamond. It closed to make way for road development.

In America the president's wife has often played a big part in official life, as shown by such powerful figures as Eleanor Roosevelt, Jackie Kennedy, Nancy Reagan and Hillary Clinton. This has seldom been the case in Britain, though critics of the presidential style of Tony Blair will point an accusing finger at his wife, Cherie, stating that she has increasingly adopted a role as a form of first lady. Whether or not this is true, people have forgotten the way that Winston Churchill acted during the war. He was the government, our sole saviour, or so it seemed. 'Good old Winnie' was not averse to using his wife as an extension of his charismatic power and she was sent on a morale boosting tour of industries vital to the war effort. On 23 and 24 April 1941 she visited Sunderland and its shipyards, giving a cheery wave to workers who appeared less than impressed with their eccentrically dressed 56 year old guest of honour. Wearsiders did not need geeing up because they worked flat out to help the country without requiring such gimmicks to motivate them. Mrs Churchill was born Clementine Hozier and was something of a society beauty when she married the then president of the Board of Trade in 1908. She provided a stable influence during Churchill's somewhat turbulent career, but she was not averse to sharing the limelight when the occasion arose. Clementine died on 12 December 1977, aged a venerable 92.

Above: With a name like Roland Hill this Inspector of Sunderland Special Constabulary could be said to have been giving the stamp of approval to the parade of officers following in his wake as he took the salute on Thanksgiving Day, 29 September 1945. They had served with distinction during the war and took their rightful place amongst the other special, voluntary and conscripted forces that had protected Britain at home and abroad during six years of hostilities. Those fighting in the air, on the seas and at the battle-front were the ones who gained the greatest publicity, but their victory could not have been achieved without the support of those who worked selflessly at home. We could not have survived without the efforts of firefighters and medical staff, nor would we have got through those dark days without the constabulary that helped keep law and order. They were also there helping out as the bombs rained down around them, helping to marshal the support services coming to the rescue of people trapped in the wreckage of their homes or protecting their property from the attention of the criminal element who had little regard for anything other than their own selfish main chance. The Specials were well named and they lived up to their soubriquet, so we saluted them in return.

It was eyes right for the men of the Royal Armoured Corps (RAC) in the Thanksgiving Day parade on 29 September 1945. Their steely determination, epitomised by the lantern jawed soldier at the head of the column, had been forged from a proud history that made the RAC the army's fist, with the Infantry forming the glove and arm, providing the punch for military strikes. The members of the Corps are the descendants of the Royal Tank Regiment who manned the first tanks, and before that the famous cavalry regiments of the line. It still had a named cavalry wing until 1939, formed from the former cavalry units that had mechanised, but this and other regiments came under the RAC banner as they also mechanised, further including former infantry battalions as numbered RAC regiments. There was hardly a spare inch of pavement not taken up by grateful, cheering crowds who paid homage to the service and sacrifice of those who had given their all in defending our little island. Those summer and autumn days of 1945 were punctuated with parades and celebrations as the general public threw off the gloom of wartime and laughed again. VE Day, VJ Day and Thanksgiving Day were just a few of the occasions when flags were waved and bunting flew.

Beamish Museum

Here is a sight to drive the politically correct mad and force them to rush off a letter to the 'Sunderland Echo' demanding that women be given more respect, for they are the subject of male exploitation. That is one view, but this bevy of beauty (and the pc lobby will not like that description) had no time for such opinions on 11 June 1953 and, now drawing their pensions, probably have not changed their minds since. They had come from across the county as winners of town and village beauty contests to compete for the prestigious title of 'Queen of Durham'. How on earth the judges managed to differentiate between charms of one compared with another no one knows, but they had to come to a decision. In time honoured tradition the MC built up the tension before the winner's name was announced over the tannoy. Beatrice Turner blushed with pride as she heard the result and took to her throne as the crown was placed on her head and a bouquet of flowers pushed into her hand. Eric Morley took beauty queens on to a global stage with his Miss World contest in the early 1950s, but he felt that he had to make the girls appear more glamorous by appearing in bathing costumes. He was wrong, as these Durham girls showed, for in their long dresses their good looks and charm shone more brightly than from any skimpy cozzie.

Beamish Museum

Above: On 16 October 1953 these earnest, God fearing women of the Salvation Army Home League were on the stage of the Salvation Army Citadel as their leader read the rallying cry and word of the Lord to the assembled audience. At one time there were only two types of women who would venture into the toughest and roughest of men's domains, the public bar. A veil can be drawn over the profession of one type, but these uniformed ladies selling the 'War Cry' occupied the other. Even the foulest of mouths remained closed when the 'Sally Army' woman walked in through the smoky haze and hard bitten dockers and shipwrights dug into their pockets to buy a paper none of them would ever open. It was a Friday night ritual and, once she had made her way from the bar, drinking resumed and the cursing continued unabated until her next visit. Sunderland's Citadel opened in 1891 on the site of the old Lyceum Theatre that had first put on a mixture of entertainment on 25 August 1852 with a production of 'Giralda', an interlude, 'The Loan of a Lover', and a farce, 'The Captain is not a Miss'. Charles Dickens once read to an audience from above the very spot where the Salvation Army logo was placed and the actor manager, Henry Irving, also trod these boards.

At first sight you might be fooled into thinking that this was another example of the havoc wrought by wartime, but the date was 14 December 1954. Joplings, on High Street West, was gearing up for the final sales push before Christmas when it was ravaged by the biggest fire seen in Sunderland during the last century. The night-time sky was illuminated as if a mammoth celebration was under way for a Guy Fawkes' party, but there was no rejoicing taking place. Millions of gallons of water were pumped from 20 fire appliances, manned by 100 fire officers, as the building blazed out of control for three hours before firefighters were able to get to grips with it. The glow could be seen 20 miles away and residents from nearby properties in the William Street area were evacuated from their homes as real fears existed that the flames could extend to them. Remarkably, considering the intense heat and great danger, no casualties were reported and the thanks for that must go to the bravery and skill of the fire crews who risked their own safety in protecting both people and property as they successfully battled to gain the upper hand. Father Christmas escaped the flames on his sleigh, carrying with him a Scrabble set on sale for the first time and on whose board he picked out the word 'thanks', scoring 13 in the process.

Flying high above the rest

The name of Rolls-Royce has been incorporated within the English language as a byword for both quality and excellence, something that no other manufacturer has been able to achieve. Quite often a vacuum cleaner is referred to as a 'hoover' or a storage flask as a 'thermos', but these are merely product labels. When a soccer player is described as the Rolls-Royce of his team we know that the commentator is offering direct praise to the individual skills of the sportsman, but is also making an indirect reference to the nonpareil class of the company that grew from the electrical and mechanical business set up by Henry Royce in 1884. In concert with Charles Rolls, a pioneer motorist and aviator, the prestigious name of Rolls-Royce was unveiled on 15 March 1906, launching the Silver Ghost, the model that was to be the first of the series of motor cars that were to be the envy of the world.

However, it is not with those magnificent machines that the plant on the Pallion Industrial Estate is concerned, though, of course, it continues to follow the company ideals of high performance and reliability with the aero engines and components manufactured there. Rolls-Royce has long been more than a car manufacturer, diversifying into the marine and aviation worlds early in the last century. The connection with Sunderland is more recent, for it was in 1966 that Bristol Siddeley Engines was acquired by Rolls-Royce Limited to form Rolls-Royce Limited (Bristol Engine Division). The factory had been used since 1951 by the Bristol Aeroplane Company for the production of pistons, sleeve cranks, main drive shafts and gears for the Hercules and Centaurus radial piston engines. This was at a time when the nation was attempting to get back on its feet after

the war and we were still living in a climate of austerity. With the hard graft of the workforce and the determination of management, the 1950s proved to be a period when the 'Great' was put back into Britain once more. As the decade progressed, order books began to fill and workers reaped the benefits of high employment and better rewards for their labours. Many of them had come from the declining shipyards and heavy engineering industries that were to come under threat from the changing

Above right: *The polishing shop (man intensive) during the 1950s.* **Right:** *The civil defence team outside the training hut, circa 1953.*

demands of the new technology of the era, the workforce soon adapted to the lighter and more exacting requirements of the manufacture of aero engine parts.

The establishing of the Bristol Aeroplane Company's aero component factory in Sunderland was assisted by a team of engineers, mainly recruited from the company's sites in Accrington and Bristol. Although some returned to Bristol after laying the groundwork, most of the others made Wearside their home and continued at the plant until they came of an age to draw their pensions. With a keen eye to the future, a recruitment programme was established to attract young people to undertake apprenticeships that would equip them with the skills required in the modern world. Additionally, building upon the experience of war work when traditional male occupations were taken on by their wives and sweethearts, women machinists were a valuable part of the team of employees. Some may have been familiar with the complexities of machining items for the home, but this was a completely different use of the terminology when applied to the work they undertook turning and refining pistons and other aeronautical parts. There was such a rapid increase in the amount of business coming in that a second factory, known as the No 2 Shop, opened in 1952. It was here that the apprentices were trained and where a toolroom was established, along with the development engine manufacturing section for the main components used in the Proteus, Orion and Ramjet engines used to power ground to air missiles. Proof that Harold Macmillan, Britain's prime minister in the late 1950s, was correct when he announced, 'You've never had it so good', when describing

the British economy, was borne out by the success being achieved at the Bristol Aeroplane Company. However, it was obviously ahead of its time, because, five years before Supermac's epoch making statement, a third factory, not surprisingly called the No 3 Shop, opened in 1954. For such growth to have been achieved in so short a time is a fine testimonial to the hard work of the employees and the entrepreneurial skills of the management. It was an inspired partnership.

In 1956, the Bristol Aeroplane Company, whilst remaining the holding company, re-organised itself into Bristol Aircraft, Bristol Cars and Bristol Aero Engines in which the Sunderland facility was included. This gave the aero engine business freedom to concentrate on aero engine manufacture. Another change took place in 1959 when in order to compete for an engine contract, Bristol Aero Engines merged with Armstrong Siddeley Motors to form Bristol Siddeley Engines Limited. Further developments were taking place around this time as there was less demand for piston engines and a greater demand for such products as discs and casings for the Pegasus and Olympic gas turbine engines that would later be used on the Harrier Jump-jet and the Concorde airliner. With the further reorganisation, when acquisition by Rolls-Royce took place, production of different types of engine components were introduced. The most significant new

Top left: Women gear inspectors in the early 1950s.
Below: The Bristol Aeroplane Company football team pictured in 1954.

parts were a range of compressor discs, for use in the highly successful Spey, two-shaft bypass engine. These parts, having a very thin diaphragm were difficult to produce on the existing machine tools, therefore to overcome this problem a new production line of Heyligenstaedt twin turning machines were installed into the plant, yet another example of keeping up to date and ahead of the competition. These machines performed so well that they are still in use today, though they have been upgraded to CNC (Computer Numerical Control).

The Sunderland facility was designated as part of the Rolls-Royce Limited Aero Engine Division in 1969, a restructuring that was not merely a cosmetic alteration of name, for it heralded a complete change in the manufacture of parts for the RB211, Avon, Tyne, Dart, Spey, Adour and Conway engines. Much of the production work on the Bristol Engine Division components was transferred to other sites as the factory at Pallion concentrated on its new work, ensuring that high standards of efficient delivery and quality were maintained. A huge investment programme pumped money into providing new machine tools, including the latest models for drilling, turning and milling. As befitting a far-seeing company, investment in people was considered as important as that made in the tools of the trade. The workforce was provided with the appropriate training opportunities to help them acquire the new skills that operating the modern machinery demanded.

Rolls-Royce has a vast tradition and experience from which to draw, having been at the forefront of the aeronautical industry since the first world war. It has not all been about making a profit, as any successful company knows that it has to consider a wider perspective than just producing a balance sheet that is in the black. Without good will and a strong reputation, those figures can so easily turn red overnight. So, it was as a tribute to his late friend, Charles Rolls, and in response to the needs of his country that Henry Royce turned his and the Company's engineering skills to aero engine design in the years leading up to the first world war.

Top right: Manufacturing engineering drawing office (notice all the drawing boards). Above right: Machining pistons, 1953. Left: A social works trip leaving from the old No1 factory

His Eagle engine was a pioneering venture that provided some 50 per cent of the aeronautical horsepower used by the allies during the 1914-18 war. So successful was Royce's design that it continued in use well into peacetime, being used on the first ever direct transatlantic flight as well as the inaugural flight from England to Australia. On both occasions the Eagle provided the power for the Vickers Vimy aeroplanes. Sadly, none of this was witnessed by his partner, Charles Rolls. He would have revelled in this aspect of the company's success because he was a bold and fearless pilot, in 1910 being the first to fly a non stop return trip across the English Channel. Tragically on June 12th of that year, during a landing manoeuvre, Rolls brought his aircraft down in a steep glide and pulled the nose up sharply. The experimental tailplane could not take the strain and disintegrated. The aeroplane plunged into the ground and Rolls died within minutes becoming the first person to be killed in an aeroplane accident. By the end of the 1920s the 'R' engine had been developed and this was used in Britain's entry to the International Schneider Trophy contest, a competition for seaplanes. It helped establish the world air speed record of 400 mph in 1931, a fabulous achievement when considering that the Wright brothers had only managed to introduce the world to the novelty of flying a mere quarter of a century before. Other records were set on land and water before Royce turned his hand to the development of the Merlin engine that lived up to the qualities of its namesake, the small powerful member of the Falcon family. But it was more than power that was needed to turn the Merlin into a world beater. It needed skill, determination and an eye for the future needs of the industry. Although Henry Royce did not live to see the project through, he had provided the impetus for the development of the engine that helped our pilots win the 1940 Battle of Britain in their Hawker Hurricanes and Superma- rine Spitfires. It was the Merlin, as much as any other engine, that helped transform Rolls-Royce from being a small player in the aero industry into a major force with which to be reckoned. Before the end of the war the company had progressed even further in this field, developing Frank Whittle's gas turbine engine. Rolls-Royce again demonstrated its ability to seize the opportunity and anticipate future markets by committing itself to this revolutionary product, one in which it quickly established a technological superiority over its rivals.

Above: *Employees' Childrens Christmas party, 1963.*
Below: *Apprentices pictured in 1965.*

Another innovative phase in the history of the company was entered in 1953 when Rolls-Royce turned its attention to the civil aviation market with its Dart engines being fitted into the Vickers Viscount airliner. It was with this step that the aircraft industry accepted that the gas turbine engine would underpin all development in the immediate future. The directors at Rolls-Royce might have been forgiven for saying, 'I told you so', but they were not ones to rest on their laurels and continued to look forward to ever more exciting ventures on the horizons. The Avon powered Comet became the first turbojet to enter transatlantic service and, in 1960, the American giant, Boeing, used the Conway in its 707, the first instance of a turbofan being used in an airliner. By the late 1960s, as the general public took to the skies in greater numbers when package holidays, intercontinental travel and business trips became more frequent, wide bodied civil airliners had to be the way forward.

Carrying more and more passengers, they also needed to be fitted with engines that could provide the necessary power, performance and reliability and Rolls-Royce launched the RB211 for the Lockheed L-1011 Tri-star

Top: *A low-roof machine shop, used in the 1960s and 70s, with machines of the same type set out in lines.*
Above: *Apprentice training school in the 1970s.*

even more. As an increasing volume of discs and casings were brought in for manufacture, a procedure of machining similar parts through a common route, using identical tooling, was organised. This cell strategy provided impressive savings in both time and money and provided the stimulus for the establishment of

jumbo jet. This three shaft turbofan concept established itself at the core of the company's family of engines and, although the 1970s brought difficult times to the country as both recession and inflation bit hard, several derivatives of the RB211 engine parts helped sustain the Sunderland site during this era.

Having left behind the three day week, industrial unrest, winters of discontent and strife of the 1970s, Britain entered the Thatcher boom years of the 1980s as the economy surged forward once more. This was also an exciting period for Rolls-Royce at Sunderland. The work rolled in again and the company committed large resources to further new machinery. It readily took on board the acknowledgement that the existing factory could not cope with the new demands placed upon it by the increase in size of aero engines and the larger machine tools. The building had a roof that was too low for the plant to function efficiently and, as this would inhibit technical advancement, a new purpose built facility was commissioned adjacent to the one then in operation.

The modern building, with its increased capacity, was formally opened on 28 June 1980 by the Mayor of Sunderland, Councillor L Harper. The roof height of 25 feet provided ample room for the new Morando Numerical Control vertical lathes that were to be utilised in the manufacture of large turbine discs. In what had now become the new No 1 Shop, a full sweep crane covered the whole of the shop floor area. Changes in working patterns helped to smooth the work in the new building

design teams, wherein engineering worked closely together with manufacturing to ensure that all newly designed parts would fit directly into this new cellular system. It had particular effect on the engine components for the Tay, V2500 and RB211 derivatives. They fitted as smoothly into their respective cells as the whole process did into acceptance as part of the initial design concept for all new and upgraded engines. This was just another example of the

Above: *The new No1 factory under construction (high roofing for modern machine tools).* ***Below:*** *Opening of the new factory, June 1980, (from left to right) Mr and Mrs D Heads, Managing Director, the Mayor and Mayoress of Sunderland, Mr and Mrs L Harper and Facility Manager, K Raine and Mrs Raine.*

company's ability in recognising a problem, addressing it and providing a solution that was an improvement to both methodology and practice that had gone before.

The company that had been taken into state ownership in the 1970s returned to the private sector in 1987, since undergoing a number of mergers and acquisitions that have helped it become the only one in Britain capable of providing the power for use on land, at sea and in the air. In 1990, Rolls-Royce formed an aero engines joint venture with the German BMW company, in January 2000 taking full control of what is now called Rolls-Royce Deutschland and Co Ltd KG. A new aero engine, the BR710, was introduced and the Pallion site was involved in the manufacture of development discs. During that last decade of the millennium there was a steady growth in production at Sunderland, with site autonomy for the manufacture of discs being established. Work that had previously to be completed at the Derby plant could now be finalised here, thanks to the installation of a curvic machining and balancing cell. Even the painting operations, formerly subcontracted or carried out by other sites, were brought in-house to complete a greater feeling of self reliance. The 1990s also saw the development of the new Trent engine, designed for the even bigger breed of new jet airliners coming into service. Several stages of disc required by the Trent are manufactured at Sunderland, as are various ones for the EJ200, SMIC and WR21 engines. By the mid 1990s, however, demand for the Tay engines declined, but the gap was filled by bringing in work from other sites. The stage 9 to 12 compressor discs for the V2500 engine, various standards of Compressor Cone and work on behalf of Hispano Suiza of France all helped to make up the shortfall and demonstrate, once again, the flexibility of Rolls-Royce, Sunderland in being able to address a potential problem before it becomes a crisis.

As the last century drew to a close the company made the £576 million acquisition of Vickers plc, bringing further capabilities under the Rolls-Royce wing. This coincided with yet more orders coming in for the engine types supported here. In addition, after many years of development, the world's most technologically advanced fighter engine the EJ200

is at last being installed on production aircraft (Eurofighter) planned for delivery to the RAF and other participating nations; Germany, Italy and Spain over the next 15 years. This, along with being involved in the development engines for the joint strike fighter of which Rolls-Royce is a key player in the proposed engine configuration. These projects help place the company in a strong position to compete on the global scene despite a continually changing market.

Above and top left: *Modern day products-discs (compressor, turbine and fan discs).* ***Top right:*** *A team of people from Rolls-Royce visiting a customer.* ***Below:*** *Pupils from Redby School looking at engine parts at Rolls-Royce.*

The work at Sunderland has more than played its part in the overall picture and can boast increasing productivity over the years along with meeting the demands of a changing technology. To ensure that the younger generation are aware of these technological advances the facility has formed a partnership with Redby School, Sunderland where it shall support pupils in engineering related areas and improve understanding of the mutual benefits to be gained between teachers and industrial personnel to

advance the future of engineering. It may all be a far cry from the modest firm set up by Henry Royce in 1884, producing electric cranes, or the company he founded with Charles Rolls 22 years later to market the cars he began building in 1904, but the basic premise has changed little. If you want to be the best, then make the best and continue to improve the product so that it remains the best. There can be little argument that Rolls-Royce, in all its guises, has continued to do just that. At Sunderland the enterprise is true to its word. With a new site infrastructure in place, combined with an ongoing and evolving improvement culture, the vision of Rolls-Royce Sunderland as first choice for disc manufacture, a centre for excellence and an employer of choice is no mirage. After all, what else would you expect from the Rolls-Royce of companies?

Above left: Today's modern fan cell, high roofed for good working conditions. Above right: A view of the manufacturing engineering office, no drawing boards, nowadays it is all PCs. Below: The Rolls Royce Facility.

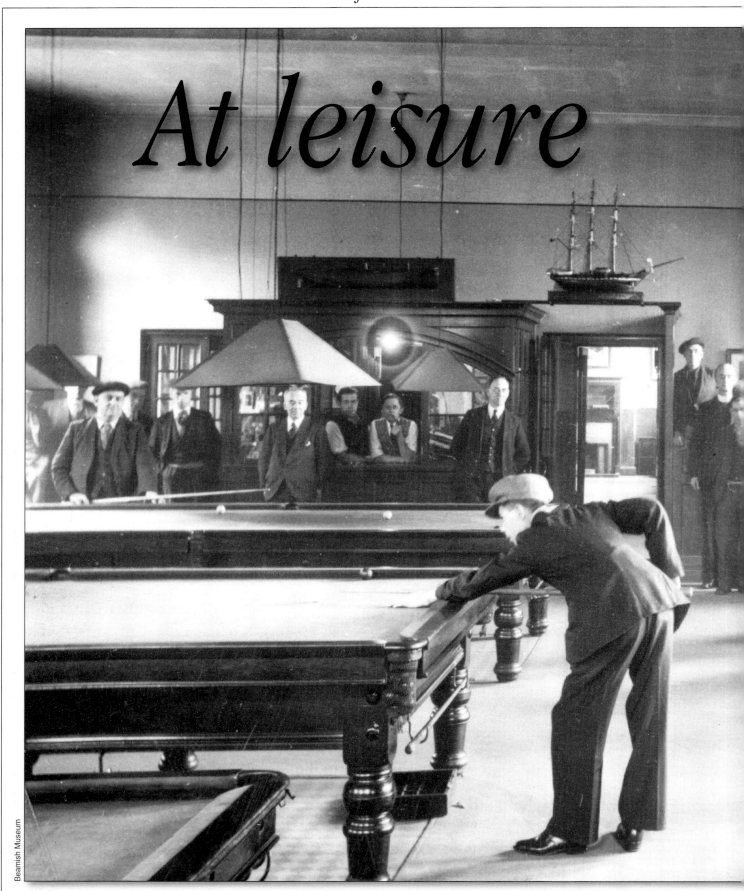

At leisure

Beamish Museum

The Mission to Seamen on Villiers Street provided a haven for men and boys where they could meet or stay out away from the temptations of the streets, with their drinking dens and unsavoury vices that led many a weak willed chap astray. Missions were established to offer moral as well as physical comfort, in a charitable effort to keep the susceptible on the straight and narrow. They variously offered reading rooms, accommodation, prayer meetings and refreshment facilities. Believing that the devil finds work for idle hands, there were plenty of recreation facilities. Ironically, dedicated snooker and billiard halls became known as signs of a misspent youth, but this Mission had obviously decided that the moral environment it provided would not encourage the betting and iniquity that led others to condemn the green baize game. Some of the men playing dominoes at the tables around the room were waiting their turn on the cloth and the best of them would have their own prized one piece cues, carefully stored in metal tubes, locked away for their personal use. They were more likely to have played billiards than snooker, for the former was the premier and more skilful game. The first professional snooker championship was not played until 1926, when Joe Davis won the princely prize of £6 10s (£6.50), and in 1931 there were only two entrants for the whole competition.

The promenade at Roker was crowded in the 1930s and 1940s even on days like this one when the weather was not at its best. Its popularity continued after the war, but competition from the continental package holiday in later years meant that scenes like this one, when the sands were covered in bodies and the steps and walkways were thronged with people, would seldom be repeated with such frequency. Seaside pleasures were varied, with amusement centres and their penny slot machines, ice cream 'stop me and buy one' sellers pushing their carts along, donkey rides, Punch and Judy shows, sandcastle competitions, hunting for crabs in rock pools and cricket matches being played to the annoyance of those snoozing in deckchairs as a six hit whistled past their ears. The promenade development was begun in the 1860s, partly as a means of providing employment during a period of recession, though not fully completed for a further 20 years. It was not immediately popular because the middle classes felt that it was too near the socially inferior masses who populated Monkwearmouth. Eventually, the attractions of the spot outweighed prejudice and crowds flocked to the sands and down the Cat and Dog steps to the area that was a time honoured sun trap. Work on Roker Pier began in 1885, with the half mile great breakwater and lighthouse being opened on 23 September 1903.

Beamish Museum

Above: Farr, the Bradford goalie, made a safe catch during the FA Cup tie at Roker Park in 1937, though there was every chance that he would be subjected to a heavy shoulder charge from an opposition forward once his feet hit the ground. In those days the 'keeper was fair game and not given the degree of protection from modern referees who will not let you so much as nod at one without blowing up for a free kick. However, Sunderland's players would not have taken many liberties because their thoughts were still with Jimmy Thorpe, the goalkeeper who died in 1936 after being kicked on the head during a game. Soccer then was a different game from the one we now know with its designer gear, massive wages and television schedules to be obeyed. Before the war men soaked their boots so that they were moulded to their feet, dubbined them carefully and laced up their ankle length sides to give them security on the heavy grounds. Every player knew his place as fullbacks were meant to clatter wingers over the touchline and halfbacks manoeuvre a sodden lump of leather through the mud for the centre forward to hammer into the net. Sunderland had one of its memorable seasons in 1937, going all the way to Wembley and lifting the Cup after a 3-1 victory over proud Preston. Captained that day by Hendon born Raich Carter, Sunderland was enjoying a spell as one of the country's top sides, having been League champions in 1935-36.

Beamish Museum

Above: The Lambton Arms at 19 Crowtree Road was one of a host of small pubs around the town centre that had few pretensions about their status. They were drinking establishments, largely the province of the male population, with little interest in anything other than the sale of alcohol. If you wanted food you went to a café, though there might occasionally have been a jar of pickled onions on the counter. Pub games were centred around cards and dominoes, with special variations of nap, don, crib and fives and threes being played. Cries of 'Ten for game', 'Morgan's orchard' and 'Double ender' meant little to the uninitiated, but were part and parcel of the language of the man about to 'peg out'. Critics of the drinking culture point to the ruin it has brought to the lives of many families and has often been the root cause of violence in the home and on the streets, but alcohol was once regarded as an essential part of our diet. It was a safer drink than milk, a beverage full of dangerous bacteria before Louis Pasteur took a hand, and even hospitals used it as part of a recovery programme. In 1823 Sunderland Infirmary recommended a daily intake of four ounces of alcohol for a five year old child, rising to a pint for a teenager.

Beamish Museum

Children love little animals, especially the ones they can handle and on which they can bestow tactile affection. Their eyes light up with joy at feeling the softness of the fur or the downy delight of the feathers and, if we old timers would only admit it, so do their parents and grandparents, or why else would we have so many pigeon fanciers and dog owners in our midst? We pretend that the family cat is just some old moggie, but we love him dearly and spend a fortune on worming tablets, anti flu injections and little treats that illustrate we are just as soft as our offspring, only we won't admit it. But there is something extra special about the first pets we had, the bunny in the hutch or the hamsters on their wheels, and what wonderfully crazy names we gave them, often reflecting popular culture of the day. Goldfish have been called Jaws and kittens christened Kylie. Further back a pair of guinea pigs was known as Starsky and Hutch, whilst after the war those budgies in the cage were Elsie and Doris or Gert and Daisy, named after popular comediennes or their characters. The children in this photograph, with their typically wrinkled socks, enjoying a day at the Durham County Show can perhaps now think back to this occasion when they stroked the rabbit and the hen, or Buttons and Bows as they wanted to refer to them.

Bird's eye view

This aerial view was taken on 3 September 1949, looking south east across Sunderland from above Trimdon Street with the electricity power station in the foreground. The scene was photographed on the 10th anniversary of the outbreak of World War II as the town was still trying to get to grips with a period of recovery that would last well into the 1950s before we could truly say that we had turned the corner. People had been promised a land fit for heroes in 1918, but it never arrived and there was less optimism for similar messages put out by officialdom this time around. But, one thing was for sure, the country had changed its attitudes and there would never again be that blind trust in our leaders who had let us down so often in the past. In 1945 we rejected the old guard who had taken us into the war and elected Clement Attlee's Labour government with its promise of a new welfare state that offered more hope for the working classes who had suffered the greatest during 1939-45. By the time of this photograph the National Health Service had been established and a number of major industries nationalised. However, there was still trouble ahead for our economy as the pound was devalued by 30 per cent, leading to an increase in the cost of living, and although clothing rationing had been abandoned such staple foods as sugar and milk were in short supply.

As the pilot steadied the plane on 20 March 1962 to take this aerial shot of the town he might have felt a pang of envy directed towards John Glenn who, just a month earlier, had been the first American to orbit the earth in his historic space flight. Mowbray Park, Sunderland's oldest, dating from 1857, was the central feature of the scene below his wings. It was extended to 18 acres in 1866 when land to the north was bought from North East Railways and an iron footbridge was built to connect the two sections. The railway can be seen curving out to the right and Binns' department store on Fawcett Street is at the right hand edge of the picture.

The building in the right hand bottom corner of Mowbray Park belonged to Sunderland Central Library, though it moved across Borough Road on 23 January 1995 as the City Library and Arts Centre. Since 1970 the Civic Centre has occupied the area to the right of the park on Burdon Road. A close look at the roads around the park show how traffic congestion was becoming problematic, with queues of cars developing at the bottlenecks at the junctions with Borough Road. Lines of cars and their choking exhaust fumes became a major headache for all towns and cities now that car ownership had become the norm rather than the privilege of the middle classes.

Beamish Museum

As Low Row starts to snake away from Bishopwearmouth Church, or St Michael's and All Angels to label it correctly, our eye moves on up the photograph to take in the view to the Wearmouth road and railway bridges that has changed since 22 March 1962, or about 7 BC (before concrete) as some would have it. Many of the properties close to the river were demolished to make way for the new ring road, begun in 1968 and designed to relieve the town centre of increasing congestion. A similar aerial view at rush hour today would show that the snarling up of the roads has been removed from the centre, but deposited on the ring road and its access points at roundabouts and the bridges. In the 70s and 80s Sunderland received its share of tower blocks and office and local government developments, usually built on rectangular lines that did away with some of the beautifully carved and cast decorative architecture created by earlier generations. Stoically, St Michael's watched it all happen around it, for it had seen change before, as might be expected from a church that had its origins in Saxon times. This Christian outpost at the time of Viking raids went on to provide a pulpit for such rectors as Simon de Landham, a future Lord Chancellor, and Robert de Geneva, who later declared himself to be Pope Clement VII and helped spark off the Great Western Schism in the Catholic Church.

On the move

Sunderland Corporation bought out Sunderland Tramways in 1899 and began the electrification of the system, running its first modernised journey on 15 September 1900 with one of its eight open topped double deckers. Covering of the cars did not begin until 1905 and a Sunday service was not introduced until 1924. This No 26 model, seen at the Grangetown terminus on 28 May 1950, was built at the Hylton Road depot as a successor to the No 99. It had four wheel trucks with a normal platform and stairs, but featured a rounded dash, twin headlights and a domed roof. With its concealed lighting and brown moquette seats with their pretty floral patterns, the No 26 provided a luxurious ride for its 64 passengers. Trams had progressed from horse drawn vehicles, through the introduction of steam on 14 September 1880 to the magnificence of this modern vehicle. The peak years were those immediately after the two world wars, for there were 459 tram employees in 1921 and 564 in 1948. None of this was of any interest to the little lad gazing past the tram because something much more riveting had captured his attention. On the gable end hoarding he could see the announcement that would shortly have had him tugging at mum's sleeve to ask her if could he go. Bertram Mills' circus was in town and there would be performing seals tooting horns, mighty elephants rising up on their back legs, pretty girls riding bareback on white horses, roaring lions being tamed and clowns driving cars that came to pieces with a loud bang. Trams were two a penny to this lad; give him the sawdust every time.

Pictured on 15 July 1953 approaching Lloyd's Bank near the Wheat Sheaf depot, the Sunderland Corporation No 4 tram had performed noble service since it was introduced in 1938. It had just passed the pub after which this corner was named. Built in 1904, the Wheat Sheaf replaced an old coaching inn and is across from the quaint lighthouse that was a copy of the real one that stood on North Pier until 1902, though the replica's light was never lit in case it confused ships at sea and encouraged them to cruise down Roker Avenue! This sleek tramcar was a far cry from the ones that first took to the streets in 1879 when just over three miles of track carried cars that were lit by smoky oil lamps and had straw thrown

on the floor during the winter months. In those early days there was friction between tram drivers and cab drivers who saw their livelihood under threat. One part of the new track ran across an established cab rank and, when cabbies refused to give way, a bout of fisticuffs brought the police rushing to the scene. Although peace was restored, relationships between the opposing factions never progressed further than grudging tolerance. Those first trams ran on single tracks, with occasional passing loops at Fawcett Street and Bridge Street. When double deckers were introduced the stairs to the upper tier restricted the drivers' nearside view, leading to several nasty accidents before the design was modified.

Below: The delivery vans proclaimed that they were decorated with the 'sign of quality' and it was a neat choice of brand name that had been chosen for the products of Joshua Wilson and Brothers, photographed on Walton Lane in 1953. The Hall-Mark title, used for the series of goods handled by this major provisions merchant, implied that it carried the stamp of excellence. Although the name was dreamed up c1900 as Hall-Mark tea and also applied to icing sugar and cereals, the company's existence goes back much further, one of its proud claims being that it served the public through the reigns of nine different monarchs. Caleb Wilson, who described himself as 'an importer of Baltic, Russian and Dutch produce, a grocer, tallow chandler, tobacco and pipe manufacturer', founded it in 1761. On his death, his four sons, the eldest of whom gave the company his name, succeeded him. Wilson's carts and vans were noticeable throughout the first half of the company's history for the teams of black horses that were used. People who lived around Walton Lane at the time when this photograph was taken might remember the piles of tea chests and crates that lay around the rear of the building. They provided a very useful source of play materials for imaginative children who took them home and revamped them as makeshift dolls' houses, soap box car chassis or garages for Dinky cars. Their parents also welcomed a free supply of firewood.

Mr R R Clark/Beamish Museum

Beamish Museum

Palmer's electrical store on St Thomas' Street had taken advertising space on the side of this tram making its way past the parade at Vine Place that had been erected in 1928 on the Durham Road. On 16 March 1953 it was radio, rather than television, that had the greatest prominence in the goods that Palmer's wished to promote. We were still part of a nation glued to 'The Archers', 'Educating Archie', 'The Goons' or 'Take it from here' rather than anything the goggle box had to offer. That was to change as the year progressed when the coronation of Queen Elizabeth II inspired us to enter the world of visual entertainment in our homes. The Sunderland Corporation tramcar No 8 had only a year left to serve on this route for it closed on 28 March 1954. Trams dated back to 1878 when the Sunderland Tramways Company had been established, laying tracks from the town to Roker, Christ Church, Tatham Street and the docks. On 28 April 1879 horse drawn trams ran from the Royal Hotel, Monkwearmouth to Roker, using a small fleet of three single deckers that each catered for 19 passengers. They operated from 9 am until 9 pm, charging a flat rate of 2d (1p) that was later reduced by half. Within 24 hours of the first journey being completed a little boy had become the first accident statistic associated with the new form of public transport, though the fault was mainly his own. He was knocked down by a passing horse and cart whilst his attention was focused on the novel sight of a tram going by.

Wartime

Below: Operation Petticoat was the code name given to the evacuation of our children from the towns and cities most vulnerable to attack from the air. As soon as war was declared the first trains pulled out of the stations and off into the countryside and to safer towns and villages, a process that continued for most of September. Pregnant women, cripples and mothers of small babies were included in the ranks of the evacuees, plus some teachers to assist with the organisation of moving a large body of people in such a short space of time. Here we can see a roll call being taken, with labelled children clutching packed lunches as though they were off on just one more school trip, though they would not usually have taken their clothes with them in a kit bag. They received a mixed reception at their billets for, whilst many were greeted with open arms and formed friendships that lasted a lifetime, others had an unhappy time as they were placed with intolerant and resentful people. These latter ones despised the 'townies' with their rough ways and, sometimes, unlucky evacuees were little more than skivvies. Little happened in Britain during the first few months of what became known as the phoney war and a mixture of the lack of seeming danger and homesickness saw many return to the bosom of their own families by Christmas.

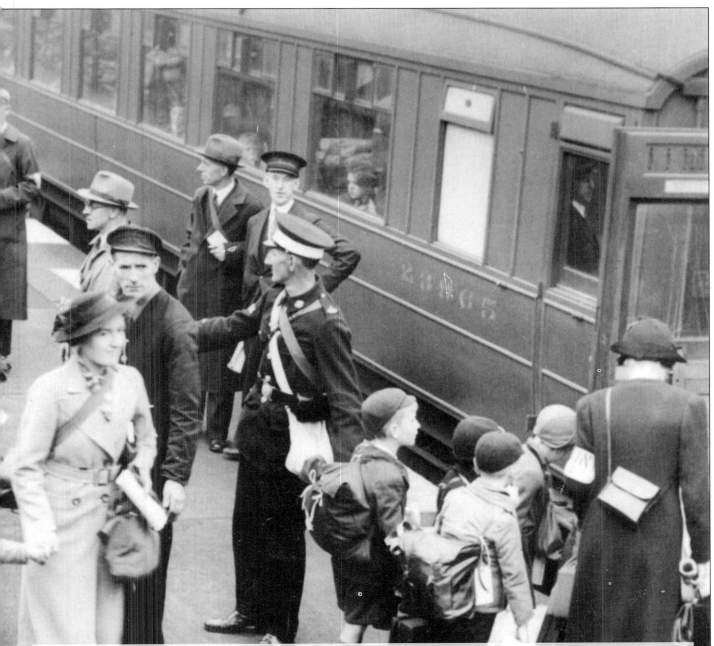

For some little tots their evacuation to safer places in more rural parts of County Durham and beyond began as a great adventure. They packed up their favourite toys, put on their luggage label styled name tags, squashed as much as they could get into haversacks and suitcases and got ready for the thrill of a ride on a train. The older children were not as excited, because they better realised that this was not the start of a magical journey but for many a separation from their parents for an indefinite period. There were a few tears shed, not only by the youngsters but also by their mums who clutched and hugged them right up to the very last minute before they had to wave goodbye. The evacuees were off to a safe haven, but the pain of separation was too much for some. They would rather take their chances as a family unit and many failed to turn up to the station, whilst others, even though they had made it to the platform, could not let go and turned on their heels and went back home. For the rest, accompanied by a handful of teachers and mothers, it was time to wave goodbye as the train got up steam and took its human cargo off into the unknown.

Busy practising with their stirrup pumps and buckets, this quartet had attracted a small knot of mildly amused onlookers. In reality this was nothing to laugh about, because this group of firewatchers had an important part to play during the war, keeping their eyes peeled for problems that they might be able to bring to the attention of the fire service, as well as lending a hand themselves. Although the equipment they displayed was primitive and hardly likely to be effectual if faced with the aftermath of a 500 lb bomb, it was the determination of these women that was especially important. Looking carefully at the people watching them that day it becomes obvious that there

are no young men in the picture, for most of that age group had joined up or were occupied in jobs essential to the war effort. Many aspects of civil defence work were undertaken by women, as were some of the jobs vacated by men who had gone off to war. They tilled the land, drove the transport and worked heavy machinery whilst others mobilised in the defence of others. The Women's Voluntary Service organised meals vans that provided assistance after an air raid, operated salvage units and ran information and advice centres. Some of them paid the ultimate price, for these women were no shrinking violets and they put themselves in areas of danger as they sought to help others in need.

Beamish Museum

Above: Fire hoses, shovels and barrows lie around amidst the rubble of the gutted Valley Road Junior School, bombed in the air raid of 10 November 1942. A new school rose from the ashes and flourishes today on Commercial Road, on the edge of the Hendon Industrial Area, but it was not to the future that we looked when faced with this grim scene. All that the police and council workmen could think about was the job to be done at that moment and thank God that this had been a night time raid or there might have been more tragic consequences. There was debris to clear and a building to be made safe, but it was work to which they had become sadly accustomed. The first attack took place on 27 June 1940, though this was a raid by a single plane and nothing to compare with the assault on Newcastle and Sunderland two months later when 63 Heinkels, supported by 21 Messerschmitt fighters, darkened the skies. There were 42 separate bombing raids on Sunderland, the last of which came on 24 May 1943. Ours was the most heavily bombed town north of Hull and it is ironic to think that Valley Road School had originally been earmarked as a temporary mortuary in case there was a large loss of life. In the months leading up to the war only pressure on the Ministry of Health enabled Sunderland to be classified as an area at risk, giving families the opportunity to join Operation Petticoat and evacuate their children to safer billets in Durham and the North Riding.

atching a parachute mine descend must have been a frightening experience for those who witnessed its journey through the air until its inevitable contact with the ground and ear splitting explosion. Just such a device fell on the railway crossing at Fulwell, not far from Seaburn Station, on 16 May 1943 during one of many raids designed to hit the transport arteries carrying vital resources to the front as part of our war effort. There was severe damage to property and two people were seriously injured, but no fatalities. In World War II we realised something of the horrors that were experienced by our troops in the 1914-18 conflict, because the war came to our own doorsteps, something that had not happened on such a grand scale before. The crater formed by this single mine measured 25 feet across and was gouged a good 10 feet into the earth. Those of us who had only heard secondhand details from fathers who had been in France and Belgium could now appreciate the damage and carnage caused by scores of such mines, shells and explosive devices. They had to suffer it on a daily basis, not occasionally as had happened here. But, life had to go on and we had 'hearts of oak', as proclaimed on the hoarding on the far side of the crossing, so out came the shovels and brushes as we cleaned up, repaired the damage and continued with our lives.

Below: This group of Land Army girls, near the Land Army Hotel on Grey Road, included Trudie Cuthbertson in the centre of the back row. She was just one of those people who were part of the greater army that Hitler forgot. They more than did their bit, for Trudie and her colleagues became the backbone of resistance in Britain to the worst that the enemy could do in trying to break our spirits. All over the country women responded to the nation's needs as they took over traditional male occupations in the factories and heavy industries. They drove ambulances and ran support and relief centres as the bombs fell around their ears during the air raids. Women donned uniforms and joined the services, providing skilful assistance in plotting troop movements and planning fighter paths for the Spitfires and Hurricanes defending our shores. The girls of the Land Army, many of whom came into the countryside from big cities with little knowledge of farm work or rural life, undertook some of the heaviest physical work. It was a shock for some to realise just how hard life was in baling hay, digging fields, lifting crops, driving tractors and getting up at all hours in foul weather to do the milking. The government tried to glamourise the work in its adverts, but the reality was much different. The work was tough and young women usually worked in isolated communities, often in old farm cottages without running water, gas or electricity. But, some friendships made during these times were worth the broken fingernails and aching backs as they continued for years after normality returned.

Right: Photographers usually like to get pretty girls to show a bit of leg when they capture them on film, but there was no flesh that Trudie Parsons, then Cuthbertson, could flash in her Women's Land Army (WLA) uniform. She would not have wanted to because hers was a practical and important role, not one to be trivialised. Trudie worked on a farm just outside the town for the last three years of World War II as a member of a vital service that kept agriculture alive and stomachs filled during those dark days. Local girls mixed with those who came from the cities to do their bit for the war effort, being paid the princely sum of one shilling (5p) an hour, but having to pay 28s (£1.40) per week board and lodging if they were billeted with a family or on a farm. It was hardly profitable work from a financial standpoint, but the benefits to the country could not be measured in pounds, shillings and pence. The WLA girls kept food production going, for without them there would not have been enough hands to till the soil, drive the tractors, care for the livestock and get in the crops. The Land Army, first called into action during the Great War, was reformed in 1939 and those who worked the land had a difficult time, especially in winter, when conditions were poor. Sometimes they had to break up the earth by hand, ready for sowing, but they tended to eat better than their town cousins as there was a plentiful supply of wild animals available. Hares, rabbits, pheasant and partridge were frequent visitors to the pot and Land Army girls had a healthy and rosy glow to their cheeks.

Beamish Museum

The Jack Crawford on the corner of Charles Street and Whitburn Street, Monkwearmouth took the full brunt of a wartime air raid that sounded the death knell for a pub that had helped slake the thirst of drinkers since the 19th century. The hostelry was dedicated to the memory of a famous figure of the Napoleonic Wars, so it was ironic that the building should meet its end because of enemy action. Jack Crawford was a local man who served in the Royal Navy on board HMS Venerable and became known as the 'hero of Camperdown' when he shinned up the mast to nail back the colours when Admiral Duncan's flag was shot away by enemy fire. The figure to the left of the pub's nameplate is a representation of Jack carrying out his gallant act and has been preserved for posterity by Sunderland Museum. Sadly, Jack did not come to a noble end, fighting the foe on some foreign sea, but at home on his own bed stricken by cholera. The atrocious living conditions and poor standards of personal hygiene, especially in the east end, made the spread of disease rampant and, in 1831-2, over 200 died on Wearside. For a while the harbour area was quarantined, but such measures came too late to save the hero of Camperdown.

Shopping spree

Looking west along Holmeside across the road bridge above the railway, the scene has changed little in this part of the city in 50 years. Although the style and nature of the shops, the public transport and the cars may have moved on, the main fabric of the street remains recognisable. In 1952 there was no Kwik Save on the left, but we can still see most of the other building, even though some of them are now a little run down and include names like the Pzazz discotheque and Sinatra's Café Bar. About half way along on the left there is a bingo hall that was still Black's Regal in 1952, perhaps the largest and swankiest of Sunderland's cinemas. It was opened on 28 March 1932 by the Mayor, Alderman EH Brown, and had a seating capacity of 2,500. The Regal was more than just a picture house for it had its own orchestra and put on stage shows until the mid 1940s and its original organist, Arnold Eagle, was so popular that he became known as 'Eagle of the Regal', going on to an illustrious career as a musical director and conductor. In later years the Regal became the Odeon, before closing its doors to movie buffs in 1982.

In 1938, looking along High Street West from Mackie's Corner, included in the group of people on the right is an elderly woman wrapped in a shawl whose face is etched with all the cares of the world. Born when Queen Victoria was in her pomp, she has lived through some difficult times that got no better for her in the 1930s. She might never have heard of Wall Street nor owned a share in her life, but the stock market crash in 1929 and subsequent world depression affected her as much as any wheeler dealer in the city. In 1930 unemployment in Sunderland stood at 11,000, but had risen to 29,000 by 1934, a figure that represented half of the working population. But it was not just the financial problem of living on Unemployment Assistance that caused grief, there was also the mental strain of despair and loss of morale that ate away at the fabric of family life. Behind the woman in the shawl we can see a mother pushing a pram, ever hopeful of what the future might bring for her offspring. That bairn could well be using a bus pass by now, having grown up into adulthood in the 1950s during an era when employment became more plentiful, though different from the reliance on shipbuilding and mining that had been the case when mum pushed the pram along High Street West all those years ago.

Above: Maynard's, on the corner of Holmeside and Waterloo Place, was a child's delight in the early 1950s, and not all those children were of school age. There was many a so called adult who could happily revert to a mental age of 10 as he or she wandered through the wonderland of toys, model cars and aeroplanes, construction kits, dolls' houses, miniature hospitals and railway sets. There were real lead soldiers, brightly painted in regimental colours, that could be added to the fort dad made last Christmas out of an old tea chest. A miniature cannon fired shells propelled by percussion caps that blasted the heads off the soldiers we had just bought, necessitating another visit to Maynard's. There were dollies that said 'Mama' when their tummies were pressed and nurses' uniforms for us to dress up in, plus toy stethoscopes with which to examine a baby brother. Airfix kits, Dinky cars, jigsaws, weaving and raffia sets abounded and budding engineers put together bridges made from Meccano to add that little something to the layout of their Hornby Dublo railway layout. Back at home you knew you were in for a long wait when granddad came to call, for he insisted on being the one to put the correct amount of methylated spirit into the little steam engine you had bought and ensuring that it all worked properly. He said we needed his know how, but we knew he was just a big kid at heart.

Wills' tobacco products, Gold Flake and Capstan, were being heavily advertised in this photograph. Do older smokers, if they have managed to last until now, remember their first drag on a Capstan Full Strength? One or two puffs before breakfast had the head reeling better than the aftermath of six pints of Vaux's Double Maxim the night before. The woman looking through the shop window at the shoes on sale at Manfield and Sons, on the corner of Bridge Street and High Street West, must have been impressed with the vast array of goods on offer, with styles to suit all tastes. The prices seem keen to us now, for one smart pair on sale at 34s (£1.70) sounds like quite a snip, but as her husband was lucky to make £10 per week, in real terms, this was quite expensive. Still, she could dream, for at least stocks were returning to the shelves on 14 November 1950, after five years of postwar economic struggle. The domed building that Manfield's occupied was an impressive sight and had long been part of the shopping drift away from High Street and Low Street towards the Bridge Street and Fawcett Street axis. In the latter years that movement has continued into the Bridges Shopping Centre and the immediately adjacent outlets, relegating the old Manfield building to supporting a couple of bargain basement shops in a now tired looking structure that is a pale shadow of its former elegant self.

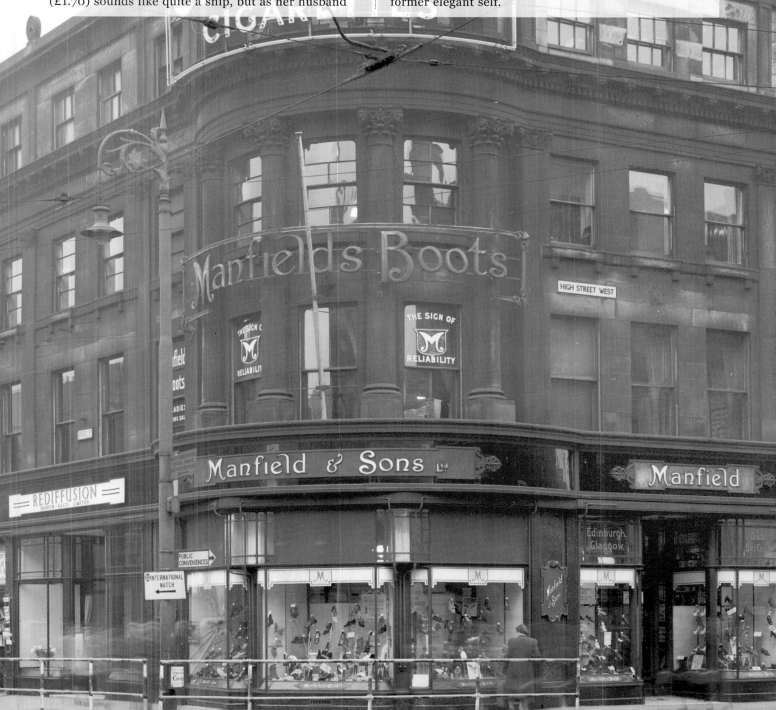

This view of Fawcett Street, seen from the corner with Borough Road in 1953, was dominated by the Northern Gas Board building, the old Town Hall and Binns' department store. Even the tram heading towards the junction was advertising the name of the establishment that had recently reopened its replace-

ment premises for the one damaged during the war on the site now occupied by a Wilkinson's store. Shoppers on the busy street and passengers on the crowded buses and tram had a lot to talk about in 1953. This was the year of the Coronation, when Queen Elizabeth II would officially take the crown in Westminster Abbey, but it was not the

only event to hit the headlines. In May Stanley Matthews, the oldest footballer to collect a cupwinner's medal, helped Blackpool beat Bolton 4-3 in a thrilling FA Cup Final at Wembley and Sir Gordon Richards rode a Derby winner at long last when Pinza galloped home ahead of the field. Cricket commentator Brian Johnston showed unusual emotion for a BBC employee when he celebrated Denis Compton hitting the runs that regained us the Ashes for the first time in 20 years. We were on top of the world, as was Edmund Hilary when he stood atop Everest in June as the spearhead of the expedition led by the Briton, Colonel John Hunt.

The swinging 60s had not fully made their mark on High Street East for Carnaby Street fashions and Mary Quant miniskirts had not been adopted by these ladies who were far happier being well wrapped up as they went about their business in the age old way, buying from shops rather than boutiques and taking a break in a tearoom and not a bistro. But changes lay ahead, even for the most traditional of Wearsiders as plans for a new town centre shopping area entered the construction stage, altering the way we filled our shopping baskets for ever more. This was to be an era when teenagers and young 20 somethings had more to spend than ever before and the retail and commercial world rubbed its hands in glee. New dance halls, fashion shops, nightclubs and restaurants appeared in the rush to empty the purses and wallets of the new breed of consumer. Social dividing lines were fudged and the young cocked a snook at the traditional values held dear by their parents, leading to much tut-tutting from older generations. Radio Caroline blared out non stop pop music from its pirate ship and the young took happily to a freer attitude to sexual mores as they adopted a 'Please please me' and 'She loves you' approach to life, whilst their mums and dads just cried 'Help'.

Above: There were still times when the old world met the new in 1953, for close to Central Station the horse and cart was about to pass the horseless carriage that had made it redundant over the preceding half a century. There were still a few occasions when the clip clop of hooves could be heard on our streets, especially when the rag and bone man came to call, collecting our unwanted bits and pieces and exchanging them for a handful of pegs or a donkeystone with which to cream the front step. Gardeners were particularly fond of a visit as the horse usually left its calling card in the middle of the road and, with a deft flick of a brush, some much needed nourishment for the roses was transferred into a bucket. Central Station had plenty of custom in the early 1950s as car ownership was not widespread and was still seen by most people as a luxury item. The cars on sale at Binns were out of the reach of even those who could afford a little runabout, for Daimler and Lanchester were aimed at the top end of the market. Anyone doubting that ownership of a Daimler was a sign of class only has to discover that one of the first to be marketed in 1889 was bought by the Sultan of Morocco and he was not short of a bob or two.

Beamish Museum

Making a living

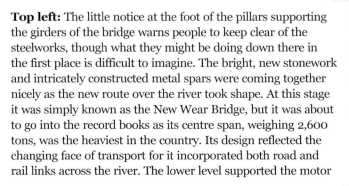

Top left: The little notice at the foot of the pillars supporting the girders of the bridge warns people to keep clear of the steelworks, though what they might be doing down there in the first place is difficult to imagine. The bright, new stonework and intricately constructed metal spars were coming together nicely as the new route over the river took shape. At this stage it was simply known as the New Wear Bridge, but it was about to go into the record books as its centre span, weighing 2,600 tons, was the heaviest in the country. Its design reflected the changing face of transport for it incorporated both road and rail links across the river. The lower level supported the motor traffic that was still a novelty in these Edwardian days, whilst the upper one carried the locomotives. The bridge was primarily built to service the coal industry, carrying trains to reach South Dock from west of Durham without the need to employ reversing manoeuvres. The enterprise turned out to be misguided as coal traffic prepared to go into a decline and ceased completely within 20 years, since when the bridge has just served road users. It had opened with a flourish on 10 June 1909 when it was revealed that Queen Alexandra, the wife of King Edward VIII, had agreed that her name could be associated with the structure.

Beamish Museum

Above: Work on the new Wearmouth Bridge in 1928 resembled a huge Meccano set as struts, girders and metalwork were bolted and riveted together in a feat of remarkable engineering. Down below work in the timber yards, coal staithes and shipyards continued unabated, but the cranes assembling the bridge would, as the 20th century continued to unfold, be employed in demolishing much of the heavy industry that had provided the foundation of Sunderland's economy. The face of Wearside would change as business centres and enterprise parks took their place. The writing was already on the wall for some of the older industries because those days of the depression had already begun to bite. After World War I the shipbuilding industry seemed to be thriving, but it was a false picture. Although 1920 was a record breaking year, with 67 ships coming out of 16 yards, rising costs caused the cancellation of many contracts in subsequent years. By 1926 output was down to just eight ships, with a mere two being launched in 1932. By this time there were only just over 2,000 employed in the shipyards with over 11,000 out of work. At least there had been employment for some as the work in this view progressed, providing the town with an updated link that was constructed around the old bridge.

Beamish Museum

The auctioneer stood on one of the 'shuggy boats' as he conducted the sale of the fairground equipment at Roker belonging to William Noble Junior in front of a crowd that contained more people who had come along out of interest than any who had any real intention of putting their hands in their pockets. Fashions change in every walk of life and entertainment is no exception. Many of us have lived through the transition from radio to television, from record player to compact disc and from dance halls to discos. Seaside and fairground fun have undergone similar, if not quite as massive, revolutions as the public seeks out faster, higher and more thrilling experiences. We now crave for theme parks and death defying rides where once we were happy with a few swingboats, a modest big dipper and a Ferris wheel. Who can forget the dangerously handsome, dark features of the lads who leapt from dodgem to dodgem collecting our sixpences or the extra twist they gave to the waltzers just to make the girls squeal that little bit louder? Their chat up lines were fairly basic, but mum had warned us about their intentions and we were able to escape at the end of a ride without anything worse than a cheeky remark coming our way. Then it was off to the boxing booth to watch some over confident youth take on the battle hardened pro with the squashed nose and cauliflower ears; all in the forlorn hope that he could win ten bob by lasting three rounds. Fat chance and fat lip too.

Beamish Museum

Above: At a quick glance this might look like sailors heaving on their ropes as they help with the mooring of some large collier on the Wear, but a more considered look at the artist's impression shows that it is work being carried out by the glassblowers at Jobling's Glassworks. This warm work demanded a high degree of patient skill only learned via a long apprenticeship, for this was not a job for a rookie. It took years to acquire the specialised knowledge and technique of a master craftsman. The Syrians invented glassblowing in the 1st century BC, where blown vessels for everyday and luxury use were produced commercially and exported to all parts of the Roman Empire. The basic techniques have changed little over 2,000 years, though in the 17th century the gaffer's 'chair', a bench with two extended arms on which the pipe is trundled to preserve the symmetry of the molten glass, came into use. The chair has since been extended to include the glassmaking crew, the gaffer and two or three assistants. James A Jobling, a businessman from Newcastle, took over the near bankrupt pressed glass firm of Henry Greener & Co on Alfred Street, Millfield in 1885, but it was his nephew, Ernest Jobling-Purser, who revitalised the business during the early 1900s. The company took a large leap forward when, in 1921, it acquired the right from the American Corning Glassworks to manufacture Pyrex. Absorbed into Corning Ltd in 1975, Jobling's continued to supply Pyrex to a worldwide market.

Below: As the 1930s drew towards their close, the death knell was also sounded for these Burleigh Street properties. It was not before time as they had long been a blight on the face of Sunderland, a breeding ground for poor health and a representation of some of the worst living conditions. The houses lacked the most basic of amenities and, although such terrible afflictions as rickets and diphtheria were largely things of the past, respiratory problems and poor nutrition remained as major factors in the lives of many residents suffering such poor living conditions. It was made all the worse by the degree of overcrowding for, despite the poverty and ill health, infant mortality fell dramatically after World War I, so maintaining large family sizes in cramped living quarters. Children often slept three or more to a bed, top to toe, with the only warmth coming from their own bodies as fuel was a luxury that had to be guarded jealously. Families often went off to the beach together, not armed with beach towels and swimming costumes but with buckets and sacks in which to collect sea coal when the tide was out. The houses here were replaced by flats that were thought to be state of the art and a pioneering example to for other councils to follow. But, today's new building is tomorrow's slum and they were swept away as part of the 1990s regeneration programme. Burleigh Street was just off High Street East, roughly in the area where Burleigh Garth is today.

The children sitting and standing around the edge of the cemetery were looking across Gill Bridge to Monkwearmouth Colliery in 1938 as below them trenches were being prepared as part of the air raid precautions that the country was beginning to make as it prepared its defences should the storm clouds gathering over Europe ever break and plunge us into another war. We now know what happened in September 1939, but 12 months earlier there were still different schools of thought as to the outcome of negotiations with the German Chancellor, Adolf Hitler. Our prime minister, Neville Chamberlain, conducted discussions in Munich and returned home waving a piece of paper that he said guaranteed peace in our time. Many believed him, but they were indulging in wishful thinking and the realists had little faith in the appeasement doctrine of the government and even less in the weasel words of the devious Fuhrer. Those who felt that war was inevitable dug trenches, practised putting on gas masks, erected shelters and carried out drills that would help them respond to an air raid or invasionary force. The children gazing across the trenches would soon be plunged into a world of blackouts, rationing and cowering in cellars and Anderson shelters as Mr Chamberlain's naÔve words came back to haunt him and the old Gill Bridge Cemetery acquired some new headstones.

ENTER SALOON THIS SIDE   ENTER TOP DECK THIS SIDE

Beamish Museum

Beamish Museum

Left: During World War I many women gained the sort of equality for which the suffragettes had been battling for years, but it was won because of the absence of male workers away fighting in the cockpit of Europe. Women moved into factories, operated heavy machinery and took over public transport, driving trams and acting as conductresses. The pattern was repeated in the 1939-45 war, with women once again rising to the challenge afforded them by the absence of their menfolk. After the first world war most women returned to the kitchen sink, but the experiences they gained in the next major conflict gave many of them the determination to hang on to jobs that men had traditionally claimed as their own. This group includes conductresses, a driver and an inspector who had no intention of being consigned to lives as 'the little women' as many of their male counterparts would have wished once peace had been declared. Although female equality with men was important, they were not averse to having discrimination within their own ranks, with a pecking order that was clearly defined. Just as male bosses wore suits and underlings had overalls, these women had clothing that reflected their standing. The inspector wore a skirt that set her above the others and the driver had a hat that put her one step on the rung above the clippies.

Above: Mrs Irwin was the manageress at the Eden Vale grocer's shop where she posed with her staff in front of the window display that attracted housewives with a mixture of the basic and the exotic. Inside they could purchase Valencia raisins or Vostizza currants whilst stocking up with rice cakes, mincemeat and Daisy White's flour at 1s 6d (7.5p) per pound. Walter Willson's, the important provisions merchant, takes us back to an era that traditionalists refer to as a time of 'real money'. Tanners, bobs, florins and half crowns were coins with their own language and even modest halfpennies and farthings had an artistic appeal with their ship and wren motifs. It was a world when computation in ounces, pounds and stones made mathematicians of all of us and all this without a calculator in sight. Shop assistants in long white coats shovelled flour from large sacks, measured out tea in quarter and half pound measures, using large scales and metal weights, and cut hunks from large cheeses on marble slabs as they exchanged cheery words with the regulars who knew they could rely on service with a smile. There were tins and boxes everywhere, with not a prepackaged, clingfilm wrapped product in sight. Butchers wore striped aprons, greengrocers had overalls with large pouch pockets and bakers appeared in starched white hats. Each shop had its own form of uniform for its employees, instantly recognisable to the practised shopper.

The number of pints contained in the barrels this line of drays normally carried is hard to determine, but there would have been enough to have kept even the hardest of drinkers busy for several months at least. Dressed in their finest livery, the draymen guided their noble horses in a procession that advertised the success of one of the north's most outstanding breweries. Just imagine how much rhubarb might have been encouraged had someone had the foresight to walk behind these handsome horses, equipped with a bucket and shovel. When Cuthbert Vaux founded his business in Pemberton Row in 1837 he would have used horses to pull his transport out of necessity, though his immediate workforce included just a single drayman. Vaux & Sons moved to Castle Street and the further expansion of its business provided work for over 200 employees by the turn of the century. The popular India Pale Ale and Maxim Ale delighted the palates of discerning drinkers, though the initial Maxim brew was a strong and heady variety that tended to send customers to sleep. As this was not good for business, for snoring suppers are incapable of reaching into their pockets to buy another draught, the potency was reduced for later Maxim Ales, whilst retaining the strong mixture as Double Maxim. Vaux Breweries is now Britain's second largest independent brewer and its modern plant is still to be found near the river.

Beamish Museum

Beamish Museum

Above: The men who had arrived from Joseph Huntley's building company in their Bedford truck had taken the opportunity to watch the angel being swung into place high above their heads as redevelopment work on the former Corders' store, now a collection of shops and offices, was well under way on Union Street on 12 June 1957. The activity was taking place opposite Central Railway Station, built in 1879 for North East Railways, but demolished in 1964. Littlewoods now occupies most of this side, though access to the new station can still be gained from here. Union Street is a short cut through from what is the now pedestrianised Market Square and the shopping complex of the Bridges Centre to the part of High Street West that is also restricted to those on foot. Looking along Union Street to High Street West in this photograph today the shops in the distance now include BHS, a butcher's and a sports shop. The slim building in the centre has kept its lettering high up on the stonework, where 'Lockharts' can be clearly read, reminding ladies of the days when you could not tell which twin had the Toni as they sat under the hairdryers whilst dizzy assistants twittered on about holidays and problems they were having with their boyfriends.

First port of call

The development of Sunderland's harbour covers a span of over 300 years. The first authenticated evidence of Sunderland as a place of maritime commerce however is contained in a charter granted by Bishop Pudsey as early as 1154.

Coal began to be exported from Sunderland at the close of the 14th century although it was not until the middle of the 17th century that this became a major local activity. In 1565 Sunderland was described in an official report as being 'in great decay of building and inhabitants'. Overshadowed by its powerful neighbour on the Tyne, and challenged by an unpromising silt ridden river and partly choked harbour, the emergence of Sunderland as a port with significant potential was bound to be difficult.

The average cargo carried by Sunderland vessels was 18 chaldrons (a chaldron of coal weighed 53 hundredweight) whilst in Newcastle the average was 58 chaldrons. The reason was simple, as one writer recorded in 1708 'There wants a pier...besides the bar is so choked up there is a

great want of water...if any storm arises at sea there is no safety in offering to go into Sunderland'. The problem was not helped by unscrupulous ships' masters who habitually dumped their ballast creating, or at least seriously contributing to the creation of, both an inner and outer bar.

In 1717 however an Act of Parliament appointing the first Commissioners of the River Wear was passed and one of their first activities was introducing fines for ballast dumping, something which would provide a steady income for more than a century.

The new commissioners undertook a programme of wharf building to stabilise the banks of the lower river and harbour in order to direct a greater force of water against the inner and outer bars. More dramatic was the building

Below: *Sunderland Harbour, from the Pier. There are many interesting details on this famous engraving of the harbour circa 1800. The wooden lighthouse burnt down on at least one occasion but at least it was easily replaced.*

of a South Pier, 1,000 feet long and 30 feet wide, built between 1723 and 1730 partly on a natural limestone foundation but with piles driven further out.

A North Pier was completed in 1795. One of the finer features of the North Pier was a distinctive 76 foot tall octagonal lighthouse erected in 1801. The result of that and other improvements was that by the 1820s Sunderland had doubled its rate of coal exports over the preceding 50 years.

But even more facilities were undoubtedly needed. In 1837 the Wearmouth Dock (North Dock) was opened having been constructed by the Wearmouth Dock Company under the authority of a Royal Charter. Nor was that the only improvement: in 1841 the North Pier was extended and one of the most remarkable engineering feats in the port's history occurred when the stone built octagonal lighthouse was undercut and moved on rails using screws and winches at 33 feet per hour to its new location 475 feet from where it had been built.

In 1846 the Sunderland Dock Act of that year led to the Sunderland Dock Company being authorised to construct docks on the south side of the river too, with the Hudson Dock opening in 1850.

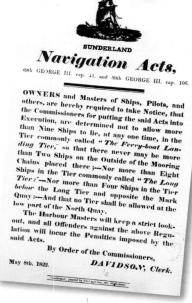

SUNDERLAND
Navigation Acts,
49th GEORGE III. cap. 41. and 59th GEORGE III. cap. 106.

OWNERS and Masters of Ships, Pilots, and others, are hereby required to take Notice, that the Commissioners for putting the said Acts into Execution, are determined not to allow more than Nine Ships to lie, at any one time, in the Tier commonly called "*The Ferry-boat Landing Tier*," so that there never may be more than Two Ships on the Outside of the Mooring Chains placed there;—Nor more than Eight Ships in the Tier commonly called "*The Long Tier*:"—Nor more than Four Ships in the Tier below the Long Tier and opposite the Mark Quay:—And that no Tier shall be allowed at the low part of the North Quay.

The Harbour Masters will keep a strict look-out, and all Offenders against the above Regulation will incur the Penalties imposed by the said Acts.

By Order of the Commissioners,
DAVIDSON, Clerk.
May 8th, 1822.

The South Dock Company had been created in 1845 with a projected capital of £225,000 and it confidently predicted a return of ten per cent. The difficult issue of whether it should be the RWC or SDC which would be entitled to the duties from vessels using the dock, and especially the sea outlet, was left unresolved. That issue would ultimately be fatal to the SDC.

In the meantime work on new groynes had begun even before legislation had been passed and from February 1847 work began on the main basin. A huge coffer dam was constructed and the work of excavation began. The excavated material was used to supplement the effects of the groynes. At the peak, in August 1849, a total of 1,200 wagons, 1,300 men and ten steam engines were in use. The main basin was completed and formally opened in the Summer of 1850.

Top: Sunderland Harbour, 1823. Particularly notable are the Pickernel lighthouse on the North Pier and the manually operated dredger to the left. The harbour was a veritable forest of masts in those days.
Above: A RWC berthing notice dated 1822.

Work then proceeded with the southern side of the basin and the sea outlet. To deal with the dangers of blocking by littoral drift, hydraulically operated sluices had been installed. The hydraulic apparatus not only operated the sluices but also the gates of the half tide basins and a railway swing bridge. At the same time the dock was extended and a timber pond added. On completion of these sections, by the end of 1856, there was an impressive 147 acre complex with 127 acres of reclaimed land. The water surface alone was 66 acres. The total cost had been £750,000.

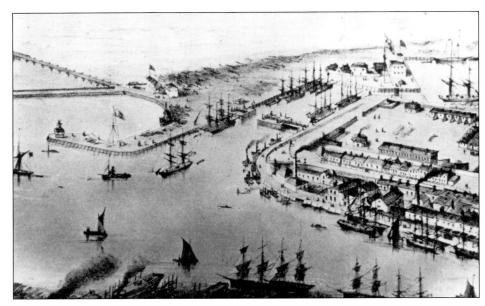

It was a considerable achievement in technological terms. Yet the economic value to Sunderland was equally impressive. Over the period 1851-58 the quantity of coal exported from the Wear rose by 56 per cent and the share of the South Dock in that rose from 16.4 per cent to 42.6 per cent.

Although the South Dock was of inestimable value to the town the South Dock Company itself did not survive for long. The unresolved dispute over the relationship between the dock and the river for the purposes of the distribution of income from dues on coal exports and shipping continued. It was impossible to reach a compromise and the result was that the SDC ran into financial difficulties and the River Wear Commissioners took it and its assets over in 1859.

More works followed: the Hendon Dock opened in 1868.

Other works took longer to complete; though the foundation blocks of the Roker Pier were laid in 1885 it was not to be completed until 1903. The building work began on a natural rock outcrop then proceeded outwards on foundations of rubble and cement. Some of the great blocks used weighed up to 56 tons each. The blocks were put into place by a massive 290 ton hydraulic crane on rails dubbed Goliath which became a town landmark. Through the whole length of the breakwater ran a subway which was to carry cables and allow safe access for maintenance work when weather conditions were bad. The final blocks were laid in place in 1902. The 2,800 feet long breakwater with its distinctive red and white granite lighthouse was officially opened on 23rd September 1903 by the Earl of Durham who placed a polished black commemorative block on the lighthouse.

It had always been intended to build a twin South breakwater. Work on the pier began in 1893. By early 1902 however a crisis point was reached because the combination of a new harbour pattern and a deeper channel had the effect of turning a much greater force of water against the old piers. The result was that alarming splits began to appear in the round head of the old North Pier which caused the original octagonal lighthouse there to tilt to such an

Top right: *South Dock, 1849 prior to the official opening of 1850. The central feature of this sketch being the barracks - of which only the street names survive today.* ***Above:*** *The opening of the South Docks, by George Hudson, 1850.* ***Left:*** *George Hudson, the Railway King, MP for Sunderland from 1845-1859.*

alarming degree that it had to be removed. Work then continued on the south breakwater until 1912 when it was decided not to proceed any further than the then 2,700 feet and finish it off with a round end. The New South Pier as it is known remains uncompleted to this day.

A significant addition to the RWC properties in this pre-first world war period was the splendid new RWC office building in St Thomas Street which was built in 1907. The volume of coal exports in that year was 4,396, 932 tons (the record of 5,498,179 tons would be reached in 1927) . The income generated and the associated status warranted more appropriate premises even though, as subsequent events would show, the rate of growth in the Wear coal export trade, if not yet its volume, had peaked.

The 20th century too was to be marked by continuing developments. In 1922 the Wear Navigation and Sunderland Dock (Consolidation and Amendment) Act was passed authorising

amongst other things the reconstitution of the River Wear Commissioners who that year acquired the North Dock. Five years later the Sunderland Corporation Act authorised the construction by the Corporation of a deep water quay on the south side of the river. The quay opened in 1934.

Further improvements were of necessity delayed by the second world war but by 1946 a post war improvement programme was put in hand. The first of these was the construction in 1948 of a new aluminium alloy bascule Bridge, the first of its kind in the world and opened by the Minister of Transport. Sadly that wonder of the Wear was condemned and demolished in 1977.

*Top: Roker Sands, circa 1900. The beach crowded in the days when people dressed in their finery to go to the seaside. **Above:** The mouth of the Wear. The huge crane Goliath can be seen in the distance, circa 1902, as the Roker Pier is well advanced but the old Pickernel lighthouse is still standing on the old north pier.*

Other post war improvements included widening the river at Folly End and a new ship repairing berth at North Dock for TW Greenwell & Co. Ltd completed in 1961.

Surprisingly, given their longevity, during the following decade the undertakings of the River Wear Commissioners would be transferred to the Sunderland Corporation.

The increasing significance of co-operation between the Sunderland Corporation and the RWC had become apparent after the first world war and had been reflected in the increasing number of members from the Corporation. That trend culminated in 1972 in the vesting of ownership and control of the Port of Sunderland in Sunderland Corporation as the Port of Sunderland Authority. In September 1972 the RWC Board met for the last time after 255 years and the formal transfer of authority took place on 1st October.

A new Port Office opened in Barrack Street in 1973, offices which would remain in use until the current offices, Quayside House, Wylam Wharf were opened in June 2000. Meanwhile in the mid 1970s M/V Aurora would be launched at Sunderland at 154,489 tons d.w. the largest vessel ever launched at Sunderland. The end of the 70s however would see Austin &

Pickersgill's covered shipyard open in Southwick and the South Docks yard closed.

Despite these developments all was not well. By 1972 the level of coal exports was down to 921,078 tons regardless of recent modernisation to the South Dock facilities. The Wearmouth Staithes had closed in 1969 and the Lambton and Hetton Staithes in 1966. Similarly the number of vessels using the port had fallen from 5,545 in 1901 to 1,568 by 1961. By 1980 the number had fallen again to just 832 vessels. The average size of vessels was however far larger and therefore the perennial problem of dredging the river would be an expensive one to deal with. Worse was to come as far as the economy of Sunderland was concerned with the ending of shipbuilding there in 1989 and the closure of the Wearmouth Colliery together with most of the other pits in the region.

Above: *Thomas Davison, one of the RWC Divers. Mr Davison was employed on the construction of the great breakwaters before 1914.* *Below:* *The Bridges. The railway bridge, designed by Thomas Harrison and built in 1879 was the last link in the Monkwearmouth Junction Line. The Road bridge which was built in 1858-1859 on the site of the original Wearmouth Bridge was designed by Robert Stephenson.*

Despite these setbacks the port continues to deal with 1.5 million tonnes of cargo each year. Of this 40 per cent is fuel and the rest is mixed cargo. Despite the disappearance of the coal trade, fuel is still a very significant element in the trade of Sunderland which acts as the major distribution point for the oil companies serving the region. Other businesses have also developed in the docks area, focusing upon metals and timber products; however the amount of space needed by these modern industries is far less than their predecessors. The greatest resource of the port is now the extensive land and water areas which have the potential to play a significant part in the regeneration of the east end and the city in general.

In 1888 journalist William Duncan wrote 'Whether it was the River Wear which made Sunderland or Sunderland that made the River Wear may be difficult to decide; but certain it is

that not one of the maritime boroughs of England has had a harder, a braver or more protracted struggle than the town at the mouth of the Wear in seeking to overcome the obstacles with which nature has encumbered its path. Compared with the great commercial rivers, the Wear is but a streamlet, yet a streamlet with a history which affords the highest encouragement to all who may feel disposed to shrink from patient persevering toil in their efforts to conquer in an unequal conflict.'

The commitment which has challenged and tamed the Wear still prevails. As the largest Local Authority owned port in Northern England Sunderland is planning for a future which will see the Port's operational area consolidated towards the Riverside and make the areas surrounding Hudson and Hendon Docks the focus for potential development.

Cargo throughput has continued to grow at about six per cent each year and the Port takes the view that its unequalled strategic position based on easy navigational access, customer oriented services and a long term development policy are wholly in tune with the markets of the 21st century. Today, whilst looking with pride to its past, the Port of Sunderland looks forward to its future with undisguised optimism.

Top: Pilot cutters on stand-by, 1995.
Above left: Loading crane parts for export, 1995.

University celebrates 100 years of higher education

Sunderland has been an important centre for education since 674 AD, when Benedict Biscop built St Peter's Church and monastery. Among its early students was a seven-year-old boy who became known to history as The Venerable Bede, a renowned scholar and teacher.

The broad sweep of river bank surrounding the ancient church of St Peter's is now the setting for the University of Sunderland's award-winning St Peter's Campus. The first stained glass ever made in England was created for St Peter's Church and the modern site is, appropriately, home to the National Glass Centre - a prestigious building in which the University's glass and ceramics teaching and research are based.

The University's modern roots lie in Sunderland Technical College, which opened at the Galen Building in Green Terrace in 1901. The local Taxation and Customs and Excise Act of 1890 paved the way for the new College, which was paid for from so-called 'whiskey money' at a cost of £27,800.

From the outset, the College had much in common with today's University, now celebrating 100 years of higher education in Sunderland. It enjoyed considerable support from local industry and from key public figures such as Mr Samuel Storey MP and councillor Dr Robert Gordon Bell, the first Chairman of Governors.

The Principal, Mr Branford, was Sunderland's Director of Higher Education and was also responsible for the School of

Below: *The Galen Building, home of Sunderland Technical College, pictured in 1940.*

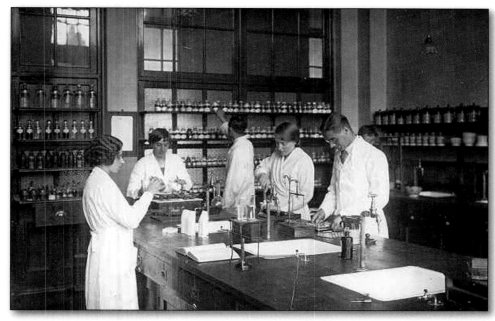

same year and the College was recognised by London University as a centre for its BEng in 1934.

During the Second World War, the College ran special courses for the armed forces and the Ministry of Labour. By 1946, the College had 59 full-time staff, 175 part-time assistants, 840 full and part-time students and 1,485 evening class students. New course development in the post-war period included the department of housecrafts, recognition of the '.... modern woman's realisation that she must have appropriate training if she is to play her part more effectively in her chosen trade, profession or in the home ....'

Art and the new Bede Collegiate School. From the start, the intention was to develop capacity and quality in order to achieve University College status.

The dynamic new College was the first in England to introduce the 'sandwich course' - enabling engineering apprentices to gain higher qualifications whilst working. By 1908, 25 engineering firms were involved in the scheme. The concept of educational progression, familiar nowadays, was already in place by 1910, when evening classes were re-structured to allow specialist study after two preliminary years.

The late 1950s saw further expansion as the College sought the status of College of Advanced Technology. As the Technical College concentrated on advanced teaching, the two local colleges of further education took over most of the non-advanced work. The College was the first educational centre in the region to install a digital computer. This hi-tech innovation apparently required a crane to haul it through the roof of the building in which it was housed - a far cry from today's laptops and palmtops.

The first great surge of expansion took place between 1919 and 1939. The Galen Building was extended between 1922 and 1930, supported by both private and public funding. In 1939, the industrialist Sir John Priestman opened the Priestman Library, with room for 10,000 books.

The building was also home to the departments of mathematics and mining. In 1921-22, departments of

In 1959, an ambitious building programme began, culminating in the opening of a new complex of buildings on Chester Road by HRH Prince Philip, Duke of Edinburgh, in 1964.

These developments meant that Sunderland's Technical College was the first in the region to offer residential accommodation at £5 per week half board. By then there were 1,750 full and part-time students, and the College was the largest of 25 regional

naval architecture and pharmacy were introduced. The pharmacy department began as a single bench in the chemistry department, but grew to become the largest in the country. The department's pioneer was a remarkable scientist, Miss Hope CM Winch. Growth in quality was soon reflected in affiliation to the University of Durham in 1930. The London University BSc pharmacy was introduced in the

colleges. In the mid-1960s, Sunderland had the largest Norwegian student body outside Norway itself, some 260 students - many of them taking marine engineering.

Top left: *Students busy at work in the early days of the pharmacy department.* ***Above:*** *Graduates pose for the annual education photograph outside the Cloisters in 1958.*

Sunderland Polytechnic was created on January 1, 1969, with a new department of education, for teacher training, established in the same year. The Polytechnic was among the first three of the 30 such national institutions, which were set up to concentrate on professional and vocational courses and develop part-time provision.

The Polytechnic brought together the Technical College with two other institutions which had played a significant role in the town - the School of Art and, later, Sunderland Training College.

A School of Art and Science had been established in 1860. By the turn of the century classes were run in the Town Hall and the small science section had been disbanded. As well as a fine art curriculum, it also ran classes in painting and decorating, stone and wood carving, photography, millinery and dressmaking. The industrial classes grew rapidly as employers paid fees for many of the students. In 1934, the College of Arts and Crafts moved to new accommodation in Ashburne House, donated by TW Backhouse.

By 1960 there were more than 1,000 students and, in 1963, the re-designated College of Art began to offer a degree-equivalent diploma in art and design and fine art. In 1982, Sunderland established the UK's first degree course in glass design and it remains a leading European centre for glass design and research.

The Training College had opened in 1908, with 70 students, male and female, and tuition fees of £10 per annum. Staff included a sergeant major to teach 'Swedish drill'. In 1922, students moved into Langham Tower in Ryhope Road, bought by the Corporation for £8,000. At the same time the College became 'women only' and remained that way until 1959. Under its last principal, Mr H Armstrong James, the Training College reached its zenith with 820 students and 80 staff.

By 1968, the Technical College ran the first interdisciplinary undergraduate degree programme outside the university sector, a BSc materials science. In 1973, it mounted the first part-time, in-service BEd in the country. By 1980, the student body had leapt to 2,294 full-time and sandwich students and 1,446 part-time students.

In 1990, Dr Anne Wright was appointed Rector at Sunderland. She then became one of the first female Vice-Chancellors of an English university when the Polytechnic gained university status. In the same year, HM The Queen granted Sunderland city status to mark the 40th anniversary of her accession to the throne.

Top right: HRH Prince Philip opening the Chester Road Campus in 1964, accompanied by Sunderland Mayoress, JE Hedley. **Above:** *The first Bachelor of Education students to complete their degrees at Sunderland in 1966.*

In 1993, HM The Queen and HRH The Duke of Edinburgh visited Sunderland and the University to celebrate. Her Majesty met University staff and saw plans for the flagship St Peter's Campus development, which has made a significant contribution to Sunderland's regeneration.

The £37m campus is now home to about half of the University's total student population of well over 14,000. Sunderland Business School opened here in 1994 and the spectacular Informatics Centre followed two years later. In April 1996, HRH The Prince of Wales laid a foundation stone to mark the official opening of the whole campus.

St Peter's plays a significant community and regional role. The 400-seat Sir Tom Cowie Lecture Theatre, named after the Sunderland businessman who is one of the University's most loyal supporters, has hosted international conferences and community musical concerts as well as student lectures.

In 1998, the Oscar-winning film producer David (now Lord) Puttnam became the University's first Chancellor in a memorable ceremony at St Peter's Campus. Lord Puttnam visits Sunderland regularly to officiate

at key events, including graduation ceremonies, as well as leading workshops for students and acting as an outstanding ambassador for the University.

Professor Peter Fidler became the current Vice-Chancellor and Chief Executive in April 1999, joining the University from Oxford Brookes University. As well as leading efforts to enhance the University's growing reputation for high quality teaching and research, Professor Fidler contributes to regional regeneration as a member of several North-East development bodies.

During the past century, Sunderland has frequently set the pace in higher education. The University continues to look forward, and work is due to start soon on the first phase of a new £20m centre of excellence for the arts, design and media at St Peter's Campus. The development's first phase will provide the latest teaching, research and commercial facilities for subjects such as digital media, creative arts, IT and entertainment. Sunderland aims to become an international powerhouse for the creative industries, with the new centre at its heart.

With grateful thanks to Stuart Miller for his research on the University's history.

Above left: *Lord Puttnam at St Peter's Campus after being installed as the University's first Chancellor in May 1998.* ***Below:*** *(Left to right)Professor Peter Fidler, University Vice-Chancellor, Sir Tom Cowie, Chairman of the University's Development Trust and Steve Cram, President of the University's Alumni Association, with plans for the new centre of excellence in arts, design and media.*

Plumbing the heights

Plumbing is an ancient craft. Its very name gives us a clue. Taking its name from the Latin word for lead the business of working with pipes goes back at least as far as the days of the Roman Empire.

Some even argue that the fall of the Roman Empire was indirectly due to plumbers: the argument goes that the Romans managed over generations to systematically poison themselves by drinking water taken into their homes via lead pipes. Well, it's one theory.

Whilst the causes for the fall of Rome may be open to dispute there can be no doubt that the Romans were into water supplies in a big way. Every hour many thousands of gallons of water flowed into the great city of Rome along aqueducts and were distributed to the populace along wood and metal piping - to public fountains for the masses and directly into the houses, villas and palaces of the wealthy.

Pipes within Roman houses were made of lead; each pipe handmade by plumbers out of sheet lead moulded round a wooden pole then soldered along their edges.

Not everyone in Rome was however scrupulous about paying their water rates.

Above: A view of the premises in the 1980s. The premises remain unchanged today but the rest of the Company is completely transformed, with modern vehicles, mobile phones and first class engineers. Below: One such engineer with over 20 years service, Steve Cobon.

The ancient writers tell us that water police had to be employed to check on unscrupulous householders who would employ equally unscrupulous plumbers to tap into the public water mains to draw free water from them.

But when did plumbing arrive in Sunderland. The answer surely is that it came along with the Roman legions in the early part of the first millennium.

Hadrian's wall may be a ruin but the knowledge which first brought piped water and central heating to the Sunderland area almost two thousand years ago remains a far more lasting testament to the skill and ingenuity of those ancient Romans and their British 'apprentices'.

One local inheritor of that tradition is Fred Stoddart Ltd of 28 Wilson Street, a Corgi registered gas installers and Member of the Institute of Plumbing. Today the company provides plumbing, heating, servicing and drain cleaning services to a wide range of clients.

Not quite two thousand years old nevertheless the firm is a long established one having been formed in 1870 making it one of Sunderland's oldest plumbing firms. The business was in the Stoddart family for generations but when the late Fred Stoddart died in 1984 it was sold to the present owners. Managing Director Barry Sanderson and Co-Director Graeme Gilligan have built up the business so much since then that it has now become one of the largest and widely recognised plumbing and heating engineers in Sunderland.

The company has been based on the Sheepfold's Industrial Estate since 1964 but prior to that was located where the Marks and Spencer's store is in the High Street West. At that time the business concentrated mainly on brewery work such as repairing and servicing hand operated beer pumps. Although Fred Stoddart Ltd is still largely associated with brewery work the company also carries out major refurbishment works for a variety of contracts which takes its employees all over the UK.

Today the firm has over 40 employees, all from the Sunderland area. As well as supporting local employ-ment the company also supports local business taking pride in buying its stock from other local firms.

And lead piping? Most readers will recall lead piping from their youth when it was still found in all the older homes. Today however lead piping has all but disappeared to be replaced by the far safer copper. When Fred Stoddart began his firm in the reign of Queen Victoria his professional skills would in many ways have been perfectly understood by his Roman professional forebears. Soldering lead piping was an art which had survived for over two thousand years and no doubt Fred, had he thought about it, might have imagined that the skill might well last another two millennia. Little could he have guessed at the changes to our lives which would occur during the 20th century with the return of central heating and indoor plumbing, and that today plumbers would be providing us with more home comforts than even a Roman Emperor could once have dreamed of.

> *The firm is a long established one having been formed in 1870, making it one of Sunderland's oldest plumbing firms.*

Below: *The management team at Fred Stoddart Ltd, 2001. From left; Steve Grant, Contracts Manager, Graeme Gilligan, Contracts Director and David Walker, Senior Estimator.*

Flying sparks

One of the best known local electrical contracting firms in Sunderland is that of George V Cummins Ltd.

The long-established business was founded, not unexpectedly, by one George V Cummins, the grandfather of one of the present directors.

The company founder was born in Byker, Newcastle. During the first world war he was an army despatch rider and after the war came to Sunderland and started work for Brantingham's electrical contractors in Norfolk Street.

Young George Cummins and his wife lived in a flat above Brantinghams and their sons George junior and Ron were born there, with their youngest son Stan coming along later.

During the second world war George worked at James A Joblings 'Pyrex' glassworks as a maintenance electrician. Between shifts however George carried on doing electrical work on his own and this was to be the start of his own business.

Later George bought a cottage in Palmer Street, Millfield and after a while moved on to Queen Street in the town centre where his business began to flourish.

Top left: *George V Cummins founder of the company.*
Above right: *An early George V Cummins Electrical Contractors Association certificate of membership.* **Right:** *A Cummins family picture, George Snr (centre), wife Mary (second right), son George Jnr (far right), daughter Bessie and son Ron (far left).*

George's three sons started working for their father as soon as they were 14, their first wages were £1 a week. Though there were breaks for National Service for George and Ron and a stint in the Merchant Navy for Stan they returned to work for their father. Not that all of them were immediately content with their lot. George junior left to work selling and maintaining vacuum cleaners before he eventually returned to the fold.

Much early business was conducted in the White Hart pub and Lockharts Cafe where many business associates

Soon the business expanded taking in more employees; the firm moved to its current premises with the compulsory purchase of Queen Street to make way for redevelopment in the early 1960s. The new purpose built premises at 26 Wilson Street North then consisted of a small office area and a large workshop/garage and a store. This is now a suite of offices with workshop and storage - and it is fully computerised with the latest estimating and computer aided design facility, accounts and payroll systems.

Not everything however is new: the firm's original bronze name plate has followed each move and is currently fixed on the inner entrance door.

would meet and share work and tall tales. The company still has a long standing association with some of these original businesses such as Scraftons builders and Stoddart's plumbers.

The firm was incorporated as a limited company in 1957 with George senior and his wife as the first two directors.

Continuity has been important, not least with the firm's staff. The company always had a reputation for good workmanship and reliability; its loyal staff tend to stay with it over many years, some leaving and returning, in many cases sons have followed their fathers and brothers into the electrical trade.

In 1977 George junior's son, the third George V Cummins, joined the business after leaving the RAF and in 1984 on his father's retirement through ill health took over his directorship; on Ron Cummin's retirement in 1988 long-standing employee Mike Stubbs joined the board as a director. Mike Stubbs had served his time and spent all his working life with the company. Stan Cummins retired in 1990. Today the company continues to prosper with the latest George V Cummins and Mike Stubbs at the controls.

Top left: *George, Stan and Ron Cummins.*
Left: *Mike Stubbs and George Cummins III.*
Below: *The George V Cummins company premises.*

Soon afterwards, due to illness the company founder retired and his three sons became the firm's directors. At that time the firm's assets included George senior's Morris Oxford car and George junior's own Morris Traveller, whilst Stan had only a bike and poor Ron had nothing more than Shanks pony. The first company vehicle was soon purchased, a second hand Post Office van which Ron used.

Today the firm has 8 vans and three cars. It's a far cry from the very earliest days when the only mode of transport was a pole-barrow pushed by hand to carry tools and equipment, then bikes came in. Many a time man and apprentice would go to job with metal conduit lengths fastened to the bicycle - the man on the bike and his apprentice trotting at the side to keep up.

Accounting for change

Award-winning Tenon Jennings Johnson is today one of the best known firms of Accountants and Business Advisors in the North East. The firm specialises in providing a service to small and medium size businesses with turnovers ranging from £1-£30 million whilst also providing services to overseas clients with investments in the UK who require monthly management accounts and assistance with managing their UK interests.

Jennings Johnson was originally a small firm of Chartered Accountants and Business Advisers formed in 1965 when Michael Johnson and Godfrey Jennings, then both sole practitioners, joined forces.

In the following 21 years mergers and acquisitions resulted in offices being acquired in South Shields, Seaham, Washington and Newcastle as well as additional office space in Foyle Street and the company being greatly strengthened by the influx of new partners including David Wrightson and Simon Lundy.

Those years also saw the beginning of the electronic revolution with the firm being the first accountancy practice in the North East to use word processors in 1978 as well as becoming the first accountants in the region to install a mini computer system.

In 1988 Michael Johnson, retired. Sadly co-founder, Godfrey Jennings, died in April 1990 just a few days before his intended retirement.

In 1998 David Wrightson also retired as a partner, but retained his links with the firm by being a part-time consultant.

A merger with John Reed & Co of South Shields followed in May 1996. The partners and staff of John Reed & Co moved into Jennings Johnson's offices at 13 Beach Road, South Shields.

Simon Lundy retired as a partner in July 2000 whilst Kevin Rooney was admitted as the last partner on 1st April 2001.

In March 2001 Jennings Johnson were awarded The Journal's Durham & Wearside Service Award in recognition of the high levels of service provided to clients, business growth, innovation, the investment made in training, personnel development and technology by the firm.
In May 2001 Jennings Johnson joined Tenon Group

Above: *Godfrey Jennings (left) and Michael Johnson, founders of the company.* ***Below:*** *The Jennings Johnson Offices.*

geographical coverage throughout the UK. In order to create a strong Tenon brand, all practices acquired by Tenon were required to drop their legacy names and on 1 December 2001 Tenon Jennings Johnson became known as Tenon.

Plc and became known as Tenon Jennings Johnson. Listed on the Alternative Investment Market of the London Stock Exchange, it is the first publicly quoted accountancy based business in the UK and all employees and partners became shareholders in Tenon as a consequence of the transaction.

The firm continues to provide a wide range of services to their clients, combining the skills developed in the 35 year history of Jennings Johnson with those found in the other offices of Tenon nationwide.

Tenon was formed with the objective of becoming the first choice provider of business services to small and medium sized business and their owners and has acquired practices in other regions to provide

Top left: Malcolm Craig receives the Durham & Wearside Services award from Caroline Theobald of Excellence North East. *Top right:* John Anderson

(front left) presents Malcolm Craig with IIP Award as some of the Partners and staff from Jennings Johnson look on.
Left: Jennings Johnson partners (back row, left to right) Philip Evans, Ian Kings, Iain Corner, Paul Lancaster, and John Payne. (Front row left to right) Tim Mallon, Malcolm Holloway, Malcolm Craig and Jean Majer.

Nothing's Nisa than this

When it came to choosing a career, Sunderland man, Herbert Jones, didn't think twice.

Born in the 'back' shop of a grocer's, he's the son of a grocer and his family has been in the grocery business since the 1890s so it was not surprising that he chose to do the same.

Depression in the 1930s and right through the second world war and into the early 1950s when food was rationed and precious coupons were exchanged for what seemed tiny quantities of food. They along with other families who lived through those anxious years became expert at cooking culinary miracles out of what was available at any one time.

How different the situation was for Herbert in the prosperous years of the 1960s and even today for Herbert and his son, who are able to sell a wide variety of fresh foods as well as grocery and household items.

He formed the company, H Jones & Son in 1958 and though there have been many difficulties and headaches on the way, and a great deal of very hard work the firm is still going strong today, now that his sons Brian, Graham and Peter are involved in the business.

It was his grandmother who started the association with the grocery trade when she operated a house window shop in her front room, moving some time afterwards to a small shop in Spelter Works Road. Herbert's father, also called Herbert was a frequent visitor to this shop but his main reason for doing so is somewhat unclear: it is true that he often bought items of food there but perhaps his chief motivation will become clear when it is revealed that he went on to marry the daughter of the shop owner.

The young couple lived in the accommodation at the back of the shop and it was here that Herbert junior made his entrance into the world. The family moved to bigger premises in Albany Terrace in 1927 and the old shop was occupied by a draper. This shop took them through the hard times of the

Above: *Founder, Herbert Jones.*
Right: *Pile it high sell it cheap, cigarettes on free sale.*

Herbert and his wife bought an additional shop in Hutton Street in 1965 but sadly their Spelter Works Road shop was threatened with demolition. A compulsory purchase order was issued by Sunderland Council in 1967 for that street and Albany Terrace and so the building came down taking many memories of the couple's early married life with it.

To celebrate the 21st anniversary of the firm in 1979, a special sale was held at the Hutton Street store. For one month all items were priced at 21 pence and all customers were given a 'birthday' ticket. Every day a birthday number was chosen and the customer holding the matching ticket received a free gift. These included perfume, aftershave and tights.

At this time the shop traded under the VG sign but only 12 per cent of its stock was VG's own brand, the rest was made up mainly of leading brand names.

Herbert Jones has always offered a good selection of lines and has specialised in fresh fruit and vegetables which were bought daily. A good selection of meat and cheese has also been a feature of the Jones's shops.

For many years a free delivery service was offered to customers spending a modest amount in the shop - this service was valued highly by many for whom carrying heavy bags of shopping would be difficult.

In 1985 another shop was opened in Vilette Road followed a couple of years later by one at 46/48 St Luke. The family business has traded under the Nisa banner since 1985, which enables them to offer a good service and pass on substantial discounts to their customers. 1991 saw the opening of the shop at 15/17 St Luke. Ever looking towards the future and seeking to offer a service which will keep their customers happy they opened a warehouse in Wellmere Road at the turn of the new century.

In the future the business will continue to offer a wide range of quality goods at attractive prices. This policy has after all been the cornerstone of Herbert Jones's success.

Above: *Peter Jones and Herbert Jones (Jnr) son and grandson of the founder.*

Children waiting to go to
unknown destinations
during Operation Petticoat,
in September 1939.

Acknowledgments

The publishers would like to thank
Beamish Photograph Library at Beamish Museum
Julian Harrop
Mr RR Clark
Sunderland Museum and Art Gallery

Thanks are also due to
Andrew Mitchell who penned the editorial text
and Steve Ainsworth for his copywriting skills